ANGLO-SAXON RELIGIOUS VERSE ALLEGORIES

Other Anglo-Saxon works
by

Louis Rodrigues

———

THREE ANGLO-SAXON BATTLE POEMS

ANGLO-SAXON ELEGIAC VERSE

ANGLO-SAXON VERSE RUNES

ANGLO-SAXON RIDDLES

SEVEN ANGLO-SAXON ELEGIES

ANGLO-SAXON DIDACTIC VERSE

———

For a complete list write to:
Llanerch Publishers
Llanerch, Felinfach
Nr Lampeter
Cardiganshire
SA48 8PJ

ANGLO-SAXON RELIGIOUS VERSE ALLEGORIES

Edited and translated by

LOUIS RODRIGUES

ISBN 1 86143 022 3

First published in 1996 by
Llanerch Publishers, Felinfach.

3

CONTENTS

PREFACE

It is worth reiterating that this final book in my series of **Anglo-Saxon Verse Specimens rendered into Modern English** is intended for a non-academic audience with no great pretensions to a profound knowledge of the complexities of Anglo-Saxon versification, syntax, diction, or whatever else the pseudo-academic reviewer feels obliged to cite have not been adequately accounted for in these renderings.

LJR, Cambridge, 1996

Introduction

There are six poems in the Exeter Book (*Guthlac A*, *Guthlac B*, *Christ I*, or *Advent Lyrics*, *Christ III*, *The Phoenix*, and *Physiologus*) and two in the Vercelli Book (*Andreas*, and *The Dream of the Rood*) which, because of their varying resemblance to the authentic works in versification, style, diction, and subject-matter of Cyn(e) wulf are sometimes considered as representing a 'School of Cynewulf'[1] whereas it was once assumed that this poet had composed all of them, or, at the very least, *The Phoenix*[2]. However, our interest in the latter and in the three known collectively as *The Physiologus* or *Bestiary* (*The Panther*, *The Whale* and *The Partridge*), has nothing to do with their authorship but with the fact that they represent a strain in Anglo-Saxon verse that may be broadly termed 'religious allegory'.[3]

Allegory is often employed as an effective method of moral and religious instruction and its devices of making truth both clear and convincing are so persuasive that Christian literature and Christian art may be considered to owe much to its pervasive influence. The medieval Church certainly found it a useful means of clarifying and stressing religious exposition. It is deeply inwrought in Scripture and in the patristic writings; and, Church carving and sculpture clearly reveal the extent to which it governed their wealth of intricate detail. It is no wonder then that Anglo-Saxon religious poetry should reflect this spirit of allegory and the many Christian symbols it created.[4]

Although the influence of allegory is evident in certain of the *Advent Lyrics* and in much of the detail of *Christ II*, or *Ascension*, there is nowhere in Anglo-Saxon verse that the creative spirit of allegory has so completely entered into both structure and substance of poetry as in these three poems in the Exeter Book: *The Phoenix*, *The Panther* and *The Whale*. *The Phoenix* consists of 677 lines, and is complete in itself. But *The Panther* and *The Whale*, transcribed later in the Exeter manuscript, are parts of an Anglo-Saxon *Bestiary*, or *Physiologus*, *The Panther* comprising lines 1-74, *The Whale*, lines 75-162. The remainder of this *Bestiary* is thought to relate to a bird identified as a partridge from the fact that these three creatures appear together, in that order, in many of the manuscripts of the

9

Continental *Physiologus*. However, the bulk of what was believed to belong to this poem is now referred to as *Homiletic Fragment III*.[5]

The Phoenix, separated in the Exeter Book, from the truncated *Guthlac B* only by the verse fragment *Azarias*, is in two parts, the first 380 lines being a very free adaptation of the Latin poem on the Phoenix attributed to Lactantius,[6] and the second 297 lines a varied allegorical interpretation of the mythical material in accordance with Christian Latin practice.

The poem begins with a description of the Earthly Paradise in which the Phoenix lives. The delineation reflects Oriental tradition, and some of the details have analogues in the Biblical Genesis ii 8-10; Ezekiel xlvii 7-9, 12; and Revelation xxii 1-2. But, in general, the landscape is that of Lactantius: a far distant plateau whose fertile soil is enriched by sweet fountains that monthly overflow, where the land is green with trees that bear in every season, where in serene, unchanging weather neither leaf withers nor fruit decays, and where nothing noxious or noisome ever intrudes. It lies near the heavenly Paradise through whose open portals may be heard the hymns of the blessed.

The Phoenix that dwells in this delightful and wondrous land is the symbol of an ancient Egyptian cult of sun-worship. The bird was associated with the rites of Heliopolis in the service of Ra, the sun god. This symbolic association of the Phoenix and the sun was central in the early myth, traces of which survive in Lactantius and in the Anglo-Saxon poem where the description of the Phoenix watching, as the stars grow dim, for the rising of the sun, is an illustrative passage. The poem continues with an elaborated picture of the bird based on the Latin text. Twelve times it indulges in its 'water-play', bathing in the pleasant fountains of Paradise and drinking of their waters.[7] Then, returning to a lofty tree it watches while the world turns beautiful in the growing sunlight. When the sun has risen high, and the earth is illumined with its blaze, then the Phoenix is impelled to adoration, winging with swift pinions into the sky, singing and carolling joyously. This vivid touch reflects clearly the spirit of the pagan myth underlying the Christian allegory.

10

There is a passage of natural, rather than Christian, implication for which the Anglo-Saxon poet is not indebted to his Latin original. In lines 243-57 he employs the symbol of seed grain for the idea of resurrection, thinking less in Christian terms than in terms of the succession in nature by which life continues through repeated rebirths in a kind of natural immortality. It is a thought that was at the heart of such natural religions as the ancient cult of sun-worship. Though it is quite distinct from the Christian development of the idea of resurrection which the poet stresses in *The Phoenix*, it lends itself easily to association with it, and is so associated in the well-known lines of 1 Corinthians xv 35-8. It finds its expression in the works of Origen, Tertullian, and other early Christian writers.[8]

From the germinal idea of the rebirth of life from sprouting seed the poet develops an extended pastoral image. Some of the pastoral detail, much like a Virgilian simile, is obviously chosen less as a constituent part of the central image than because of its easy and natural association with it. But the poetic whole is sensitively written. It is the most graceful simile in **The Phoenix**; its artistry lies in its deft evocation of the pastoral scene: the gathering and storing of grain in the harvest; the wealth of food hoarded for the months of frost and snow and winter's furious might; the return of the warm sun of springtime, the symbol of life; and once again the sowing of the grain to sprout and grow into new harvests. It is a brief, but expressive painting of the pastoral scene through the changing seasons of nature. But it grew in the poet's mind from the thought of sprouting seed and the rebirth of life.

The burning and rebirth of the Phoenix is closely imitated from Lactantius, except in one important respect considered later. At the end of every thousand years the aged bird flies to a remote region of Syria where it lodges in a lofty tree, fairest of all on earth. There in a season of clear, unclouded weather, when the winds are hushed and the sun shines hot, the Phoenix builds a nest from fragrant herbs and spice-bearing sprigs and blossoms. As the bird sits on its nest the heat of the sun kindles it into flame, and in a steam of sweet odours the Phoenix is consumed. But the ashes of the pyre fuse into the likeness of an apple from which grows a wondrous fair worm, as if it comes from an egg. From this develops first an eagle's

11

young, then a full-grown eagle, then a bird of many brilliant hues, as it was before. The Phoenix is reborn.

The one respect in which the Anglo-Saxon poem differs markedly from Lactantius in this account of the bird's death and rebirth has to do with the ashes of its former body. In Lactantius the Phoenix gathers the remains of bone and ash and with oil, frankincense and myrrh moulds them with its beak into a ball. It carries this ball to Heliopolis and there offers it upon an altar in the Temple of the Sun. Obviously, this detail of the pagan myth cannot be brought into accord with the Christian allegory for which the Anglo-Saxon poet is employing the legend. In his rehandling of the material, therefore, he suppresses references to Heliopolis and this rite of sun-worship. The Anglo-Saxon Phoenix gathers together the remains of its former body and blends them with savoury herbs, but carries them back to its native dwelling in the Earthly Paradise and there buries them.

There is in the Anglo-Saxon poem another much less important, but interesting, suppression of the material from Lactantius. In the description of the building of the funeral nest the Latin poet has listed the names of various oils and ointments which the Phoenix uses in fashioning its nest: cinnamon and balm, odorous acanthus, incense-gum and cassia, nard and myrrh. The Anglo-Saxon poet, perhaps because of the intrusive Eastern flavour of these names, has replaced the list with a general, but widely inclusive, reference to the 'sweetest things,| winsome herbs and forest fruits', and to the 'sanctifying scents| and the noblest fruits of earth'.

In the second half of the Anglo-Saxon *Phoenix*, we have explicit interpretation of the Christian allegory of the bird's death and resurrection. The flight of the Phoenix from the Earthly Paradise to the remote region of Syria is the loss of Eden by Adam and Eve and the Fall of Man. The lofty tree in which the Phoenix nests is God's grace and mercy to men. The sweet spices and fragrant herbs which are used in the building of the nest are the words and deeds of righteousness. These Christian virtues are particularized by the poet; God's warrior is one who is faithful in prayer and constant in almsgiving, avoiding evil, keeping the law, seeking strength from the Lord. 'These,' says the poet, 'are the roots,| herbs, plants that the wild bird culls| far and wide beneath the sky| for its dwelling-

12

place.' The flames that burn the Phoenix are the fires of Judgment. The rebirth of the phoenix is the soul's resurrection to eternal life.

However, as is not unusual in a poem of this type, the spirit of allegory is not to be bound in unvarying patterns. Here and there the equations of the allegory are altered, and the implications changed. Thus, in lines 508-14, and again in 552-61, the thought is of man's resurrection by the grace of God. But, in lines 646-7, the Phoenix is explicitly identified with Christ, and the fine description of its return to the Earthly Paradise attended by rejoicing flocks of all the race of birds[9] lends itself easily to an allegory of the Ascension.[10]

The use of the Phoenix as an allegorical symbol of man's faith in immortality has roots in the Book of Job where a reference to the bird is implicit in Chapter xxix 18. And it is to the Book of Job that the Anglo-Saxon poet specifically appeals for authority as he ends his allegory. He is describing the eventual fires of Judgment. They shall hold no terror for the faithful. For blessed souls, coming from their earthly exile, shall bring with them the 'sweet scent| of words and works'. They shall be adorned with glory and shall live in light. 'Let none of the race of men presume,'| exclaims the poet, 'that with lying words I compose my lay,| write my verse. Listen to the wisdom|of Job's songs.' The eighteen lines that follow[11] are directly elaborated from two passages in Job, one of which [12] is the assertion of Job's faith in resurrection set forth in the well-known verse: 'For I know that my Redeemer liveth and that He shall stand at the latter day upon the earth; and though after my skin worms destroy this body, yet in my flesh shall I see God.'

The animal in the Anglo-Saxon poem of **The Panther**, as in the Greek *Physiologus*, wears an air of medieval strangeness quite the contrary to that of *The Whale*. This, in part at least, results from the qualities assigned to the Panther in the allegorical rôle he is to play. In the opening lines he is shown to be gentle and kind, amiable and well-disposed to all except the Dragon, against whom he wages eternal warfare. When the beast has had his fill, he slumbers until the third day, when he rises glorified from sleep. From the mouth of the Panther there issues a melody and a fragrance 'sweeter and stronger than all the scents of flowering herbs and forest fruits'.

13

Men throng the roads in their desire to follow that fragrance.

As in his original, the poet hastens to unravel the allegory for his readers lest they be misled: the Panther is a symbol of Christ and His love for all, except only for the Author of evil. His sleep, and rising again on the third day, are Christ's death and Resurrection. The melody and fragrance that issue from His mouth are the Gospel of God's grace to mankind. The multitudes that throng the roads, pouring out of city and town to follow the fragrance, are the faithful who believe in Him.

It has been suggested that the original, seemingly inappropriate, choice of the Panther to represent Christ, may have been derived from the Septuagint text of Hosea v 14, where the word 'panther' held the place of 'lion' and 'young lion' of the Authorized Version. In any case, once the beast was chosen, the allegory was firmly imposed upon him. The effect is an impression of quaint and curious lore as if one were listening to old travellers' tales of far away and long ago.

The realistic description of **The Whale** contrasts markedly with the allegorical pretence of *The Panther*. For the Great Whale provides his own allegory, and has done so from the days of the legends that reappear in the tales of Sinbad the Sailor right down to the days of Melville and Moby Dick. The legend of the Whale as set forth in the Anglo-Saxon *Physiologus* is undoubtedly of very early date, and there is at least one mark of confusion and contamination in the text of the fable in the Exeter Book. The disappearing island on which the sailors land and kindle a fire, only to have it sink beneath their feet and plunge them suddenly down into the depths, is in the Greek *Physiologus* not a whale, but a huge sea-monster known as the shield-turtle. In the Anglo-Saxon poem the disappearing island is similar to that of the Greek original, but it is plainly identified by the poet as a whale. Yet somewhere behind the material which the Anglo-Saxon poet uses, the great sea-turtle still lurks, for the name *Fastitocalon*, by which the whale is called in the Anglo-Saxon poem, seems clearly a corruption of the Greek name for the shield-turtle.[13]

Not only is the Anglo-Saxon sea-monster called a whale, but the description is unmistakable. The element that is chiefly stressed is

14

the huge size of the sea-beast as he swims with open jaws, who, by a sweet odour lures into his cavernous mouth whole schools of smaller fish. In this matter of the Whale's size, the Anglo-Saxon *Physiologus* is quite in accord with ancient legend. Strabo and Pliny greatly exaggerated the size of whales, and later writers such as Basil and Ambrose compared them to mountains and islands.

The appearance of the Whale as it lies like an island motionless and partly exposed at the surface of the sea is described with detail that again seems to hint at old tradition. The Anglo-Saxon poet tells us that 'His shape is like a rough stone, | as if great sea-weeds, girt | by sandbanks floated by the shore, | so that seafarers suppose | their eyes behold an isle.' These details of appearance seem cognate to the description in Sinbad's first voyage of the great fish on which 'the sand has accumulated so that it has become like an island, and trees have grown upon it'. In the Anglo-Saxon poem the sailors moor their high-prowed ships by anchor ropes 'to that false land'.[14] Disembarking, they encamp without thought of peril and kindle a fire. The flames leap high and the sea-weary men are filled with joy. When the Whale, 'skilled in treachery', feels that the sailors are firmly established, suddenly 'the ocean'-spirit | dives down with his prey | into the salt wave, seeks the depths, | and in the death-hall tries to drown | ships and crews.'

The poet's translation of the allegory is generally similar to that given in the Greek *Physiologus*, but in the Anglo-Saxon version of the fable it is an enlarged significance and a broader application to life that is stressed. In the Greek original the image of the deceiver who drags the unwary down to the depths is from Proverbs v 3-5, where the reader is warned against the luring wiles of the harlot. 'Her feet go down to death; her steps take hold on hell.' But, the author of the Greek fable, directly addressing his reader, is quick to add the more general warning: 'If thou shalt depend upon the hope of the devil, he will plunge thee with himself down to the hell of fire.'

It is this interpretation of the allegory that is stressed in the Anglo-Saxon poem. The Great Whale is Satan. The jaws which he snaps on the unwary are the gates of hell, the yawning Hell-mouth represented in the drawings of the Junius MS that was used so often

15

later on the medieval stages of the mystery and miracle play. The Whale's sweet odour is the lure of worldly pleasures, the lusts of the flesh. The seductive wiles of Satan, and his victims' spiritual blindness mistaking evil for good and danger for safety, are the prelude to that final, sudden plunge to the depths of hell.

The Phoenix

The Phoenix

Hæbbe ic gefrugnen   þætte is feor heonan
eastdælum on   æþelast londa,
firum gefræge.   Nis se foldan sceat
ofer middangeard   mongum gefere
5   folcagendra,   ac he afyrred is
þurh meotudes meaht   manfremmendum.
Wlitig is se wong eall,   wynnum geblissad
mid þam fægrestum   foldan stencum.
Ænlic is þæt iglond,   æþele se wyrhta,
10   modig, meahtum spedig,   se þa moldan gesette.
Ðær bið oft open —   eadgum togeanes
onhliden hleoþra wyn —   heofonrices duru.
Þæt is wynsum wong,   wealdas grene,
rume under roderum.   Ne mæg þær ren ne snaw,
15   ne forstes fnæst,   ne fyres blæst,
ne hægles hryre,   ne hrimes dryre,
ne sunnan hætu,   ne sincaldu,
ne wearm weder,   ne winterscur
wihte gewyrdan,   ac se wong seomað
20   eadig ond onsund.   Is þæt æþele lond
blostmum geblowen.   Beorgas þær ne muntas
steape ne stondað,   ne stanclifu
heah hlifiað,   swa her mid us,
ne dene ne dalu   ne dunscrafu,
25   hlæwas ne hlincas,   ne þær hleonað oo
unsmeþes wiht,   ac se æþela feld
wridað under wolcnum,   wynnum geblowen.
   Is þæt torhte lond   twelfum herra,
folde fæðmrimes,   swa us gefreogum gleawe
30   witgan þurh wisdom   on gewritum cyþað,
þonne ænig þara beorga   þe her beorhte mid us
hea hlifiað   under heofontunglum.
Smylte is se sigewong;   sunbearo lixeð,
wuduholt wynlic.   Wæstmas ne dreosað,
35   beorhte blede,   ac þa beamas a

18

The Phoenix

I have heard tell there lies far hence,
in eastern parts, the loveliest of lands,
famed among folk. That expanse of earth
is not accessible to many potentates
5   across the world; for, it is set apart
from sinful men through the might of God.
Lovely that land, delightfully dowered
  with earth's sweetest scents;
matchless that isle; noble the Maker,
10   proud, rich in power, who stablished that land.
There Heaven's portals ever stand open
with songs of rapture revealed to the blest.
That plain is winsome: green woods spread
under the skies. There nor rain, nor snow,
15   nor frost's breath, nor fire's blast,
nor hail's fall, nor rime's fall,
nor sun's heat, nor ceaseless cold,
nor warm weather, nor wintry shower
work harm a whit, but the plain endures
20   unscathed and sound. That lovely land
blooms with blossoms. No hills or mountains
there stand steep, nor stony cliffs
rise high, as here with us;
no dells, no dales, no mountain-caves,
25   no mounds, no dunes, nor aught unsmooth,
lie there; but that pleasant plain
thrives beneath the sky, blooms blissfully.
    That radiant land, that region, is twelve
cubits higher (so sages from their studies
30   tell us wisely in their writings)
than any of the hills which here with us
rise brightly under the heavenly stars.
Serene is that plain: the sunny groves shine,
the winsome woods; fruits do not fall,
35   bright blossoms, but the trees ever

grene stondað, swa him god bibead.
Wintres ond sumeres wudu bið gelice
bledum gehongen; næfre brosniað
leaf under lyfte, ne him lig sceþeð
40   æfre to ealdre, ærþon edwenden
worulde geweorðe. Swa iu wætres þrym
ealne middangeard mereflod þeahte,
eorþan ymbhwyrft. þa se æþela wong,
æghwæs onsund, wið yðfare
45   gehealden stod hreora wæga,
eadig, unwemme. þurh est godes;
bideð swa geblowen oð bæles cyme,
dryhtnes domes, þonne deaðræced,
hæleþa heolstorcofan, onhliden weorþað.
50   Nis þær on þam londe laðgeniðla,
ne wop ne wracu, weatacen nan,
yldu ne yrmðu ne se enga deað,
ne lifes lyre, ne laþes cyme,
ne synn ne sacu ne sarwracu,
55   ne wædle gewin, ne welan onsyn,
ne sorg ne slæp ne swar leger,
ne wintergeweorp, ne wedra gebregd,
hreoh under heofonum, ne heardra forst,
caldum cylegicelum, cynseð ænigne.
60   Þær ne hægl ne hrim hreosað to foldan,
ne windig wolcen, ne þær wæter falleþ,
lyfte gebysgad, ac þær lagustreamas,
wundrum wrætlice, wyllan onspringað
fægrum flodwylmum. Foldan leccaþ
65   wæter wynsumu of þæs wuda midle;
þa monþa gehwam of þære moldan tyrf
brimcald brecað, bearo ealne geondfarað,
þragum þrymlice. Is þæt þeodnes gebod,
þætte twelf siþum þæt tirfæste
70   , lond geondlace lagufloda wynn.
Sindon þa bearwas bledum gehongne,
wlitigum wæstmum. Þær no woniað o,

20

stand green, as God bade them.
Winter and summer alike the wood
is laden with fruit. Leaf shall not fade
under the sky nor fire scathe
40   ever, ere the end comes
to the world. As once the water's rush,
the sea-flood, whelmed all middle-earth,
earth's circuit, then that noble plain
by the grace of God stood all secure,
45   happy, unhurt, no whit harmed
by the billowy rush of those wild waves.
Thus it shall flourish, till the fire comes,
the Judgment of God, when graves
shall yawn, death-dwellings of men.
50   There is no loathsome foe in that land,
no weeping or pain or sign of woe,
no age or anguish or narrow death,
no loss of life or onset of evil,
no sin or strife or misery,
55   no pressure of want or lack of wealth,
no sorrow or sleep or sore disease,
no wintry squall or stormy weather
fierce under heaven; no bitter frost
with freezing icicles smites any man.
60   There no hail or hoarfrost falls to earth,
no wind-blown cloud; no water falls
driven by gusts, but there the streams,
wondrous strange, gush welling forth;
fair fountains, from the forests' midst,
65   winsome waters, irrigate the land;
every month from the earth's turf
they gush sea-cold, traverse the grove
gloriously in season. It is God's behest
that twelve times through that glorious land
70   the joyous water-floods should flow.
The groves are girt with blossoming,
beautiful fruits; the forest's ornaments,

21

halge under heofonum, holtes frætwe,
ne feallað þær on foldan fealwe blostman,
75 wudubeama wlite, ac þær wrætlice
on þam treowum symle telgan gehladene,
ofett edniwe in ealle tid
on þam græswonge grene stondaþ,
gehroden hyhtlice haliges meahtum,
80 beorhtast bearwa. No gebrocen weorþeð
holt on hiwe. Þær se halga stenc
wunaþ geond wynlond; þæt onwended ne bið
æfre to ealdre ærþon endige
frod fyrngeweorc se hit on frymþe gescop.
85 Ðone wudu weardaþ wundrum fæger
fugel feþrum strong, se is fenix haten.
Þær se anhaga eard bihealdeþ,
deormod drohtað; næfre him deaþ sceþeð
on þam willwonge þenden woruld stondeþ.
90 Se sceal þære sunnan sið behealdan
ond ongean cuman godes condelle,
glædum gimme, georne bewitigan,
hwonne up cyme æþelast tungla
ofer yðmere estan lixan,
95 fæder fyrngeweorc frætwum blican,
torht tacen godes. Tungol beoþ ahyded,
gewiten under waþeman westdælas on,
bideglad on dægred, ond seo deorce niht
won gewiteð; þonne waþum strong
100 fugel feþrum wlonc on firgenstream
under lyft, ofer lagu locað georne,
hwonne up cyme eastan glidan
ofer sidne sæ swegles leoma.
Swa se æþela fugel æt þam æspringe
105 wlitigfæst wunað wyllestreamas,
þær se tireadga twelf siþum hine
bibaþað in þam burnan ær þæs beacnes cyme,
sweglcondelle, ond symle swa oft
of þam wilsuman wyllgespryngum

22

holy under heaven, never wither there;
nor do fallow flowers that grace the trees
75   fall to earth; but there, in wondrous wise,
the boughs on the trees are ever lade
with fruit, fresh through all time.
Green on that grassy plain there stands,
gaily garnished by God's holy might,
80   the brightest of groves. No breach of hue
mars the holt; there sacred fragrance fills
the land; never shall it suffer change
to the fullness of time, ere He who first
shaped it shall end His ancient work.
85   A wondrous fair fowl, strong of wings,
which is called Phoenix, inhabits that wood.
This unique being there holds its home,
brave of heart; never shall death harm
it in that pleasant plain, while the world endures.
90   There it gazes on the sun's going
and comes face to face with that gleaming gem,
God's candle, and watches eagerly until
the fairest of stars, the Father's ancient work,
God's radiant token, ornately glinting,
95   comes up from the east,
over the billowy sea. The stars are hid,
whelmed under waves in the west,
dimmed at dawn, and the dusky night
steals darkly away; then, strong in flight,
100   the bird, proud of plumage, longingly looks
out over the ocean, under the sky,
until the gleam of heaven comes gliding
up from the east, above the broad sea.
So the noble bird, changeless in beauty,
105   haunts welling streams at the water-spring;
twelve times the blessed creature there
bathes in the brook, ere that beacon comes,
heaven's candle, and ever as oft, at every bath,
cold as the ocean's surge, it sips

23

110 brimcald beorgeð   æt baða gehwylcum.
Siþþan hine sylfne   æfter sundplegan
heahmod hefeð   on heanne beam,
þonan yðast mæg   on eastwegum
sið bihealdan,   hwonne swegles tapur
115 ofer holmþræce   hædre blice,
leohtes leoma.   Lond beoð gefrætwad,
woruld gewlitegad,   siþþan wuldres gim
ofer geofones gong   grund gescineþ
geond middangeard,   mærost tungla.
120   Sona swa seo sunne   sealte streamas
hea oferhlifað,   swa se haswa fugel
beorht of þæs bearwes   beame gewiteð,
fareð feþrum snell   flyhte on lyfte,
swinsað ond singeð   swegle toheanes.
125 Ðonne bið swa fæger   fugles gebæru,
onbryded breostsefa,   blissum remig;
wrixleð woðcræfte   wundorlicor
beorhtan reorde,   þonne æfre byre monnes
hyrde under heofonum,   siþþan heahcyning,
130 wuldres wyrhta,   woruld staþelode,
heofon ond eorþan.   Biþ þæs hleoðres sweg
eallum songcræftum   swetra ond wlitigra
ond wynsumra   wrenca gehwylcum.
Ne magon þam breahtme   byman ne hornas,
135 ne hearpan hlyn,   ne hæleþa stefn
ænges on eorþan,   ne organan,
swegleoþres geswin,   ne swanes feðre,
ne ænig þara dreama   þe dryhten gescop
gumum to gliwe   in þas geomran woruld.
140 Singeð swa ond swinsað   sælum geblissad,
oþþæt seo sunne   on suðrodor
sæged weorþeð.   Þonne swiað he
ond hylst gefeð,   heafde onbrygdeð,
þrist, þonces gleaw,   ond þriwa ascæceð
145 feþre flyhthwate; fugol bið geswiged.
Symle he twelf siþum   tida gemearcað

24

110 the winsome waters of the spring.
     Then after its water-play, it proudly
     betakes itself to a lofty tree,
     whence, most easily, it may observe
     time's eastern passage, when heaven's taper,
115 that lamp of light, serenely shines
     over the tossing sea. Earth is embellished,
     the world made fair, when the glorious gem,
     most famed of stars, over the sea's sweep,
     illumines the land throughout the world.
120   As soon as the sun high overtops
     the salt-streams, then this glorious bird
     pale grey flies from that forest-tree,
     and, swift of wing, it soars aloft;
     makes music and sings towards the sky.
125 Then so sweet is the bird's song,
     its heart exalted, exulting in joy,
     it varies its song with clearest voice
     more wondrous than ever a son of man heard
     below the heavens, since the High King,
130 Creator of glory, founded the world,
     heaven and earth. The music of its hymn
     is sweeter than all song-craft, more beautiful
     and more winsome than any melody;
     nor trumpets, nor horns, nor sound of harp,
135 nor voice of any man on earth,
     nor strain of song, can equal that sound;
     nor organ's peal, nor swan's plume,
     nor any delight that God has devised
     to gladden men in this gloomy world.
140 So it sings and makes melody, blest with joy,
     until the sun has sunk again
     in the southern sky; it is silent then,
     and falls to listening; it lifts its head,
     intrepid, sage in thought; and thrice it shakes
145 its feathers, swift in flight; the bird is mute.
     Ever it marks the hours twelve times,

25

dæges ond nihtes.   Swa gedemed is
bearwes bigenga,   þæt he þær brucan mot
wonges mid willum   ond welan neotan,
150   lifes ond lissa,   londes frætwa,
oþþæt he þusende   þisses lifes,
wudubearwes weard,   wintra gebideþ.
Ðonne bið gehefgad   haswigfeðra,
gomol, gearum frod,   grene eorðan
155   aflyhð, fugla [wyn],   foldan geblowene,
ond þonne geseceð   side rice
middangeardes,   þær no men bugað
eard ond eþel.   Þær he ealdordom
onfehð foremihtig   ofer fugla cynn,
160   geþungen on þeode,   ond þrage mid him
westen weardað.   Þonne waþum strong
west gewiteð   wintrum gebysgad
fleogan feþrum snel.   Fuglas þringað
utan ymbe æþelne;   æghwylc wille
165   wesan þegn ond þeow   þeodne mærum,
oþþæt hy gesecað   Syrwara lond
corðra mæste.   Him se clæna þær
oðscufeð scearplice,   þæt he in scade weardað,
on wudubearwe,   weste stowe,
170   biholene ond bihydde   hæleþa monegum.
Ðær he heanne beam   on holtwuda
wunað ond weardað,   wyrtum fæstne
under heofumhrofe,   þone hatað men
fenix on foldan,   of þæs fugles noman.
175   Hafað þam treowe forgiefen   tirmeahtig cyning,
meotud moncynnes,   mine gefræge,
þæt se ana is   ealra beama
on eorðwege   uplædendra
beorhtast geblowen;   ne mæg him bitres wiht
180   scyldum sceððan,   ac gescylded a
wunað ungewyrded   þenden woruld stondeð.
      Ðonne wind ligeð,   weder bið fæger,
hluttor heofones gim   halig scineð,

26

by day and night; so it is decreed
that the grove's denizen may there enjoy
the plain at will, partake of bliss,
150   of life and joy, and the land's delights,
until this guardian of the forest grove,
has lived a thousand years of this life.
When the grey-plumed one grows weak,
aged, old in years, the finest of fowls
155   flees the green earth, the luxuriant land,
and then seeks out a spacious tract
of middle-earth, where no men live,
as its dwelling and domain; there, in its might,
it reigns supreme over the race of birds,
160   exalted in their midst, and for a while
dwells in the desert; then, strong in flight,
westwards it goes, swift of wing,
burdened with years. Birds throng about
the noble one, each keen to be
165   vassal and slave to the glorious lord,
until it seeks the Syrians' land
with a large band. The chaste bird there
hastens from them, that it may hold
a lonely spot in the shade of a grove,
170   concealed and hid from the crowd of men.
There in the wood it bides and dwells
in a lofty tree, secure in its roots
beneath heaven's roof, which people call
'Phoenix' on earth, from this bird's name.
175   The mighty King, the Maker of mankind,
has granted that tree, so I have heard,
that of all the trees upon earth's tract
that rear their lofty boughs,
this blooms brightest; nothing bitter
180   may wickedly scathe it, but, ever shielded,
it shall bide unharmed while the world remains.
When the wind is hushed, the weather fair,
and heaven's holy gem shines bright,

beoð wolcen towegen,   wætra þryþe
185   stille stondað,   biþ storma gehwylc
aswefed under swegle,   suþan bliceð
wedercondel wearm,   weorodum lyhteð,
ðonne on þam telgum   timbran onginneð,
nest gearwian.   Bið him neod micel
190   þæt he þa yldu   ofestum mote
þurh gewittes wylm   wendan to life,
feorg geong onfon.   Þonne feor ond neah
þa swetestan   somnað ond gædrað
wyrta wynsume   ond wudubleda
195   to þam eardstede,   æþelstenca gehwone,
wyrta wynsumra,   þe wuldorcyning,
fæder frymða gehwæs,   ofer foldan gescop
to indryhtum   ælda cynne,
swetes under swegle.   Þær he sylf biereð
200   in þæt treow innan   torhte frætwe;
þær se wilda fugel   in þam westenne
ofer heanne beam   hus getimbreð,
wlitig ond wynsum,   ond gewicað þær
sylf in þam solere,   ond ymbseteð utan
205   in þam leafsceade   lic ond feþre
on healfa gehware   halgum stencum
ond þam æþelestum   eorþan bledum.
Siteð siþes fus.   Þonne swegles gim
on sumeres tid,   sunne hatost,
210   ofer sceadu scineð   ond gesceapu dreogeð,
woruld geondwliteð,   þonne weorðeð his
hus onhæted   þurh hador swegl.
Wyrta wearmiað,   willsele stymeð
swetum swæccum,   þonne on swole byrneð
215   þurh fyres feng   fugel mid neste.
Bæl bið onæled.   Þonne brond þeceð
heoredreorges hus,   hreoh onetteð,
fealo lig feormað   ond fenix byrneð,
fyrngearum frod.   Þonne fyr þigeð
220   lænne lichoman;   lif bið on siðe,

28

when clouds are scattered, and water-floods
185   lie stilled, when every storm
is hushed under heaven, the weather's warm lamp
shines from the south, sheds its light upon men,
then it begins to build in the branches,
to fashion its nest. Great is its need then,
190   through its mind's urging, urgently
to turn senility to life,
take on fresh youth. Then far and near
it gleans and garners the sweetest things,
winsome herbs and forest fruits,
195   for its dwelling-place; every sweet perfume
of goodly herbs, which the glorious King,
Father of all creatures, created on earth,
most fragrant under the firmament,
for the blessing of men. There itself it bears
200   those radiant treasures into the tree;
there in the waste the wild bird builds
a house at the top of that lofty tree,
delightful and winsome, and dwells there itself
in that solarium; and in the leafy shade
205   surrounds its body and wings on every side
and all about with sanctifying scents
and the noblest fruits of earth;
eagerly awaits its fate. When in summertime,
the sun, heaven's gem, most hotly shines
210   above the shade, scans all the world,
fulfils its fate, then its home becomes
heated by the radiant sky;
the plants grow warm, the pleasant dwelling reeks
of sweet scents, and in that glowing heat,
215   both bird and nest are burnt in the fire's grasp.
     The pyre is kindled; then flame engulfs
the sad one's home; it hastens fierce:
pale flame consumes, and the Phoenix is burnt,
aged with past years; then fire devours
220   the frail frame; life, the fated one's soul.

fæges feorhhord, þonne flæsc ond ban
adleg æleð. Hwæþre him eft cymeð
æfter fyrstmearce   feorh edniwe,
siþþan þa yslan   eft onginnað
225   æfter ligþræce   lucan togædre,
geclungne to cleowenne. Þonne clæne bið
beorhtast nesta,   bæle forgrunden
heaþorofes hof;   hra bið acolad,
banfæt gebrocen,   ond se bryne sweþrað.
230   Þonne of þam ade   æples gelicnes
on þære ascan bið   eft gemeted,
of þam weaxeð wyrm,   wundrum fæger,
swylce he of ægerum   ut alæde,
scir of scylle. Þonne on sceade weaxeð,
235   þæt he ærest bið   swylce earnes brid,
fæger fugeltimber;   ðonne furþor gin
wridað on wynnum,   þæt he bið wæstmum gelic
ealdum earne,   ond æfter þon
feþrum gefrætwad,   swylc he æt frymðe wæs,
240   beorht geblowen. Þonne bræd weorþeð
eal edniwe   eft acenned,
synnum asundrad. Sumes onlice
swa mon to ondleofne   eorðan wæsmas
on hærfeste   ham gelædeð,
245   wiste wynsume,   ær wintres cyme,
on rypes timan,   þy læs hi renes scur
awyrde under wolcnum;   þær hi wraðe metað,
fodorþege gefeon,   þonne forst ond snaw
mid ofermægne   eorþan þeccað
250   wintergewædum. Of þam wæstmum sceal
eorla eadwela   eft alædan
þurh cornes gecynd,   þe ær clæne bið
sæd onsawen. Þonne sunnan glæm
on lenctenne,   lifes tacen,
255   weceð woruldgestreon,   þæt þa wæstmas beoð
þurh agne gecynd   eft acende,
foldan frætwe. Swa se fugel weorþeð,

30

is about to fare forth; the funeral fire
burns flesh and bone; yet, after some time,
life returns to it anew,
when the cinders, congealed into a ball,
225   begin to combine together again,
after the fire's fury. Then that brightest of nests,
the brave bird's dwelling, is clean destroyed
by the blaze. The corpse grows cold,
the bone-frame is broken, and the burning dies.
230   Then, out of the pyre, an apple's likeness
is afterwards found among the ashes,
from which a worm waxes, wondrous fair,
as though it had emerged from eggs,
gleaming from the shell. In the shade it grows,
235   fashioned first as an eagle's young,
a handsome fledgling; still further then
it blissfully burgeons, until in form
it is like an old eagle, and after that
adorned with feathers, just as it was at first,
240   brightly bedecked; then its flesh is all
renewed, reborn,
sundered from sins; somewhat the same
as men at the harvest, at reaping-time,
for sustenance bring home
245   the fruits of earth, pleasant fare,
ere winter's coming, lest a shower of rain
destroy them under the clouds; they find
joy of feasting there, when frost and snow,
with mighty power, deck the earth
250   with winter-weeds. The wealth of men
shall sprout forth from those fruits again
by nature of the corn, which is first sown
as a mere seed; then the sun's gleam
in spring awakens the signs of life,
255   the world's wealth, so that the fruits,
earth's adornments, according to their kind,
are born again. Thus the bird,

31

gomel æfter gearum, geong edniwe,
flæsce bifongen. No he foddor þigeð,

260 mete on moldan, nemne meledeawes
dæl gebyrge, se dreoseð oft
æt middre nihte; bi þon se modga his
feorh afedeð, oþþæt fyrngesetu,
agenne eard eft geseceð.

265 Þonne bið aweaxen wyrtum in gemonge
fugel feþrum deal; feorh bið niwe,
geong, geofona ful, þonne he of greote his
lic leoþucræftig, þæt ær lig fornom,
somnað, swoles lafe, searwum gegædrað

270 ban gebrosnad, æfter bælþræce,
ond þonne gebringeð ban ond yslan,
ades lafe, eft ætsomne,
ond þonne þæt wælreaf wyrtum biteldeð,
fægre gefrætwed. Ðonne afysed bið

275 agenne eard eft to secan.
Þonne fotum ymbfehð fyres lafe,
clam biclyppeð, ond his cyþþu eft,
sunbeorht gesetu, seceð on wynnum,
eadig eþellond. Eall bið geniwad

280 feorh ond feþerhoma, swa he æt frymþe wæs,
þa hine ærest god on þone æþelan wong
sigorfæst sette. He his sylfes þær
ban gebringeð, þa ær brondes wylm
on beorhstede bæle forþylmde,

285 ascan to eacan. Þonne eal geador
bebyrgeð beaducræftig ban ond yslan
on þam ealonde. Bið him edniwe
þære sunnan þegn, þonne swegles leoht,
gimma gladost, ofer garsecg up,

290 æþeltungla wyn, eastan lixeð.
Is se fugel fæger forweard hiwe,
bleobrygdum fag ymb þa breost foran.
Is him þæt heafod hindan grene,
wrætlice wrixleð, wurman geblonden.

32

grown old after years, is young again,
clothed in flesh. It eats no food,
260 no meat on earth, save that it tastes
a little honey-dew, which often falls
at midnight, by which the noble bird
nurtures its life, until it seeks again
its ancient dwelling, its own abode.
265 When the bird, proud of plumage, grows
up among the roots, its life is renewed;
young, full of grace, then, out of the dust,
it gathers its body, which fire once disfigured,
the remains of burning, artfully assembles
270 the fragmented bones, after the fire's force,
and brings together again
bones and ashes, relics of the pyre,
and rolls up that spoil of death in herbs,
richly adorned. It will then be impelled
275 to seek its own abode once more.
Then it grasps in its talons, clasps in its claws,
the fire's residue, and joyously seeks
its home again, its sunny haunts,
its blessed homeland. All is renewed,
280 life and feather coat, just as it was at first,
when triumphant God first set
it on that noble plain. It brings its bones
there which the fire's surge had once
engulfed with flame upon the funeral pile,
285 its ashes too. Then the valiant bird
buries bones and ashes all together there
in that land of rivers. The symbol of the sun
is renewed for it, when heaven's light,
brightest of jewels, best of noble stars,
290 shines from the east over the sea.
The bird is fair to behold: in front
bright with varied hues round the breast:
its head is green behind,
wondrously varied, mixed with purple;

295 Þonne is se finta   fægre gedæled,
sum brun, sum basu,   sum blacum splottum
searolice beseted.   Sindon þa fiþru
hwit hindanweard,   ond se hals grene
nioþoweard ond ufeweard,   ond þæt nebb lixeð
300 swa glæs oþþe gim,   geaflas scyne
innan ond utan.   Is seo eaggebyrd
stearc ond hiwe   stane gelicast,
gladum gimme,   þonne is goldfate
smiþa orþoncum   biseted weorþeð.
305 Is ymb þone sweoran,   swylce sunnan hring,
beaga beorhtast   brogden feðrum.
Wrætlic is seo womb neoþan,   wundrum fæger,
scir ond scyne.   Is se scyld ufan
frætwum gefeged   ofer þæs fugles bæc.
310 Sindon þa scancan   scyllum biweaxen,
fealwe fotas.   Se fugel is on hiwe
æghwæs ænlic,   onlicost pean,
wynnum geweaxen,   þæs gewritu secgað.
Nis he hinderweard,   ne hygegælsa,
315 swar ne swongor,   swa sume fuglas,
þa þe late þurh lyft   lacað fiþrum,
ac he is snel ond swift   ond swiþe leoht,
wlitig ond wynsum,   wuldre gemearcad.
Ece is se æþeling   se þe him þæt ead gefeð.
320   Þonne he gewiteð   wongas secan,
his ealdne eard,   of þisse eþeltyrf.
Swa se fugel fleogeð,   folcum oðeaweð,
mongum monna   geond middangeard,
þonne somniað   suþan ond norþan,
325   eastan ond westan,   eoredciestum,
farað feorran ond nean   folca þryþum
þær hi sceawiaþ   scyppendes giefe
fægre on þam fugle,   swa him æt fruman sette
sigora soðcyning   sellicran gecynd,
330 frætwe fægran   ofer fugla cyn.
Ðonne wundriað   weras ofer eorþan

34

295 its tail is handsomely pied,
part brown, part crimson, part cunningly speckled
with glittering spots; the wings
are hindward white, and the throat green,
downward and upward, and the bill gleams
300 like glass or a jewel; its jaws are bright,
both inside and out; the mien of its eye
is strong, in aspect most like a stone,
a brilliant gem, when in a foil of gold
it is set by the craft of smiths.
305 About its neck, like a circlet of sunlight,
woven of feathers, is the brightest of rings;
its belly below is wondrous fair,
bright and beauteous; the crest above,
across the bird's back, is splendidly joined;
310 its shanks and fallow feet with scales
are covered. In aspect, the bird
is wholly peerless; most like a peacock,
winsomely mature, of which writings tell.
It is neither sluggish, nor slothful,
315 nor dull, nor torpid like certain birds
that wing their way slowly through the air,
but it is brisk and swift, extremely light,
lovely and winsome, and marked out for glory.
Eternal is the Prince who grants it that bliss.
320 When it sets out from this earth to seek
the plains, its ancient dwelling-place,
as the bird flies, it is seen by folk,
by many men throughout middle-earth.
Then they flock from south and north,
325 from east and west, in banded hosts;
in crowds they come from far and near,
where they behold God's grace revealed
fair in that fowl as the true King of victories
in the beginning ordained for it a nobler nature
330 and fairer adornments, beyond the family of birds.
Then men throughout middle-earth admire

wlite ond wæstma,   ond gewritu cyþað,
mundum mearciað   on marmstane,
hwonne se dæg ond seo tid   dryhtum geeawe
335 frætwe flyhthwates.   Ðonne fugla cynn
on healfa gehwore   heapum þringað,
sigað sidwegum,   songe lofiað,
mærað modigne   meaglum reordum,
ond swa þone halgan   hringe beteldað
340 flyhte on lyfte;   fenix biþ on middum,
þreatum biþrungen.   Þeoda wlitað,
wundrum wafiað,   hu seo wilgedryht
wildne weorþiað,   worn æfter oþrum,
cræftum cyþað   ond for cyning mærað
345 leofne leodfruman,   lædað mid wynnum
æþelne to earde,   oþþæt se anhoga
oðfleogeð, feþrum snel,   þæt him gefylgan ne mæg
drymendra gedryht,   þonne duguða wyn
of þisse eorþan tyrf   eþel seceð.
350 Swa se gesæliga   æfter swylthwile
his ealdcyðþe   eft geneosað
fægre foldan.   Fugelas cyrrað
from þam guðfrecan   geomormode
eft to earde.   Þonne se æþeling bið
355 giong in gerardum.   God ana wat,
cyning ælmihtig,   hu his gecynde bið,
wifhades þe weres;   þæt ne wat ænig
monna cynnes,   butan meotod ana,
hu þa wisan sind   wundorlice,
360 fæger fyrngesceap,   ymb þæs fugles gebyrd.
Þær se eadga mot   eardes neotan,
wyllestreama   wuduholtum in,
wunian in wonge,   oþþæt wintra bið
þusend urnen.   Þonne him weorþeð
365 ende lifes;   hine ad þeceð
þurh æledfyr.   Hwæþre eft cymeð
aweaht wrætlice   wundrum to life.
Forþon he drusende   dead ne bisorgað,

36

its beauty and form, and their writings set it forth,
and they shape it in marble by hand,
whenever the day and the hour reveal to men
335   the splendours of the swift-flighted bird.
Then the race of birds press round on every side in bands;
draw near from far-flung ways; with song they praise
and with loud voices glorify that noble bird;
and in a circle they surround that holy bird
340   in its flight aloft; the Phoenix in the midst,
thronged about with crowds. The people look;
they gaze in wonder, marvel how the faithful band,
flock after flock, do homage to the wild bird,
mightily proclaim and praise as king,
345   the cherished lord, and joyfully lead
the prince to his dwelling, until the lone being
flies off, swift of wing, so that the joyous company
cannot follow it. Then the delight of men departs
from this earth's turf to seek its home.
350   Thus the blessed bird, after a time of death,
goes back to its ancient home,
that lovely land. The birds return,
mournful of mood, to their abode,
from the brave hero. Then the prince
355   remains young in its dwelling. God only knows,
the almighty King, what its gender is,
female or male; no one of humankind
knows it, only the ordaining Lord,
how wondrous are the facts,
360   the ancient decree, concerning this bird's birth!
There the blessed one may enjoy its abode,
the welling streams in the woodlands,
and dwell in the plain until a thousand years
have run their course. Then comes to pass
365   the ending of its life; the pyre engulfs
it with its kindled fire; yet, strangely stirred,
it wondrously returns to life.
Wherefore, drooping, it does not fear death,

37

sare swyltcwale, þe him symle wat
370 æfter ligþræce lif edniwe,
feorh æfter fylle, þonne fromlice
þurh briddes had gebreadad weorðeð
eft of ascan, edgeong weseð
under swegles hleo. Bið him self gehwæðer
375 sunu ond swæs fæder, ond symle eac
eft yrfeweard ealdre lafe.
Forgeaf him se meahta moncynnes fruma
þæt he swa wrætlice weorþan sceolde
eft þæt ilce þæt he ær þon wæs,
380 feþrum bifongen, þeah hine fyr nime.
Swa þæt ece lif eadigra gehwylc
æfter sarwræce sylf geceoseð
þurh deorcne deað, þæt he dryhtnes mot
æfter geardagum geofona neotan
385 on sindreamum, ond siþþan a
wunian in worulde weorca to leane.
Þisses fugles gecynd fela gelices
bi þam gecornum Cristes þegnum
beacnað in burgum, hu hi beorhtne gefean
390 þurh fæder fultum on þas frecnan tid
healdaþ under heofonum, ond him heanne blæd
in þam uplican eðle gestrynaþ.
Habbaþ we geascad þæt se ælmihtiga
worhte wer ond wif þurh his wundra sped,
395 ond hi þa gesette on þone selestan
foldan sceata, þone fira bearn
nemnað neorxnawong, þær him nænges wæs
eades onsyn, þenden eces word,
halges hleoþorcwide, healdan woldan
400 on þam niwan gefean. Þær him niþ gescod,
ealdfeondes æfest, se him æt gebead,
beames blede, þæt hi bu þegun
æppel unrædum ofer est godes,
byrgdon forbodene. Þær him bitter wearð
405 yrmðu æfter æte ond hyra eaferum swa,

38

dire dissolution, for it always knows
370 that after the fire's force there is renewed
existence, life after death,
when from its own ashes, it is speedily restored,
born again as bird, and grows young afresh
beneath the sheltering sky. It is itself
375 both son and dear father, and ever, too,
the heir again of its former remains.
The mighty Lord of mankind granted that
it should so wondrously become again
the same as it was formerly,
380 clothed with feathers, though fire carry it off.
Thus each of the blessed chooses for himself
through dark death that eternal life,
after painful exile, that he may enjoy,
after his lifetime, the gifts of the Lord
385 among eternal joys, and thenceforth ever
dwell in glory as guerdon for his deeds.
The nature of this bird is much alike
the chosen ones, Christ's followers;
it shows to folk how through the Father's aid,
390 they hold beneath the heavens
bright joy in this terrible time, and gain
happiness in the heavenly home.
We have learned that the Almighty wrought
man and wife through His marvellous might,
395 and then set them in the finest
of earth's regions, which the sons of men
call Paradise; there they had no lack of bliss
in that new delight, whilst they were willing
to heed the Eternal One's behest,
400 the Holy One's decree. There hatred did them harm,
the old foe's spite, who proffered them food,
fruit of the tree, so that foolishly they both
partook of the apple; against God's will,
ate what was forbidden. Bitter their sorrow
405 after the eating, and their children's too;

39

sarlic symbel   sunum ond dohtrum.
Wurdon teonlice   toþas idge
agolden æfter gylte.   Hæfdon godes yrre,
bittre bealosorge.   Þæs þa byre siþþan
410   gyrne onguldon,   þe hi þæt gyfl þegun
ofer eces word.   Forþon hy eðles wyn
geomormode   ofgiefan sceoldon
þurh nædran niþ,   þa heo nearwe biswac
yldran usse   in ærdagum
415   þurh fæcne ferð,   þæt hi feor þonan
in þas deaðdene   drohtað sohton
sorgfulran gesetu.   Him wearð selle lif
heolstre bihyded,   ond se halga wong
þurh feondes searo   fæste bityned
420   wintra mengu,   oþþæt wuldorcyning
þurh his hidercyme   halgum toheanes,
moncynnes gefea,   meþra frefrend,
ond se anga hyht,   eft ontynde.
        Is þon gelicast,   þæs þe us leorneras
425   wordum secgað,   ond writu cyþað,
þisses fugles gefær,   þonne frod ofgiefeð
eard ond eþel,   ond geealdad bið.
Gewiteð werigmod,   wintrum gebysgad,
þær he holtes hleo   heah gemeteð,
430   in þam he getimbreð   tanum ond wyrtum
þam æþelstum   eardwic niwe,
nest on bearwe.   Bið him neod micel
þæt he feorh geong eft   onfon mote
þurh liges blæst   lif æfter deaþe,
435   edgeong wesan,   ond his ealdcyðþu,
sunbeorht gesetu,   secan mote
æfter fyrbaðe.   Swa ða foregengan,
yldran usse,   anforleton
þone wlitigan wong   ond wuldres setl
440   leoflic on laste,   tugon longne sið
in hearmra hond,   þær him hettende,
earme aglæcan,   oft gescodan.

40

a sorry feast for their sons and daughters;
their greedy teeth became their bane;
retribution followed guilt. They bore God's wrath,
bitter baleful sorrow. Their children ever since
410   have paid for it, because they ate that food
against the Eternal One's command. So, mournful of mood,
they were destined to forsake that land's delight,
through the serpent's hate, when it artfully seduced
our parents in those days of yore,
415   by its guileful spirit, so that far from there,
in this vale of death, they sought to dwell
in drearier abodes. For them the better life
was hid in darkness, and the hallowed plain,
through the fiend's guile, was firmly closed
420   for many years, until the King of glory,
mankind's Joy, Consoler of the weary,
our only Hope, through His coming hither
opened it to the holy once again.

    Most like to this, by what scholars tell
425   us in words, and writings reveal,
is this bird's journey when, old and wise,
it leaves home and land and is grown old.
Weary of mood, weighed down with years, it flies
to where it finds the lofty shelter of the holt,
430   wherein with twigs and choicest herbs
it builds a new abode,
a nest in the grove. Great is its desire
that it receive, through fire's blast,
its youth again, life after death,
435   be young anew: that it might seek
its former home, its sunlit haunts,
after its fiery bath. Thus those who went before,
our parents, left that lovely plain behind
and that precious seat of glory,
440   in all its beauty, and made the long journey
into the grasp of evil foes, where their enemies,
miserable monsters, oft harmed them.

Wæron hwæþre monge, þa þe meotude wel
gehyrdun under heofonum halgum ðeawum,
445   dædum domlicum, þæt him dryhten wearð,
heofona heahcyning, hold on mode.
Ðæt is se hea beam in þam halge nu
wic weardiað, þær him wihte ne mæg
ealdfeonda nan atre sceþþan,
450   facnes tacne, on þa frecnan tid.
Þær him nest wyrceð wið niþa gehwam
dædum domlicum dryhtnes cempa,
þonne he ælmessan earmum dæleð,
duguþa leasum, ond him dryhten gecygð,
455   fæder on fultum, forð onetteð,
lænan lifes leahtras dwæsceþ,
mirce mandæde, healdeð meotudes æ
beald in breostum, ond gebedu seceð
clænum gehygdum, ond his cneo bigeð
460   æþele to eorþan, flyhð yfla gehwylc,
grimme gieltas, for godes egsan,
glædmod gyrneð þæt he godra mæst
dæda gefremme; þam biþ dryhten scyld
in siþa gehwane, sigora waldend,
465   weoruda wilgiefa. Þis þa wyrta sind,
wæstma blede, þa se wilda fugel
somnað under swegle side ond wide
to his wicstowe, þær he wundrum fæst
wið niþa gehwam nest gewyrceð.
470   Swa nu in þam wicum willan fremmað
mode ond mægne meotudes cempan,
mærða tilgað; þæs him meorde wile
ece ælmihtig eadge forgildan.
Beoð him of þam wyrtum wic gestaþelad
475   in wuldres byrig weorca to leane,
þæs þe hi geheoldan halge lare
hate æt eortan, hige weallende
dæges ond nihtes dryhten lufiað,
leohte geleafan leofne ceosað

42

Yet there were many who served their Maker
under the heavens with holy rites,
445 with glorious deeds, so that the Lord,
heaven's high King, was gracious to them.
That is the high tree, wherein the holy
now have their home, where none of the old
foes can harm them at all with their venom,
450 the token of guile, in this perilous time.
There the Lord's champion builds him a nest,
by glorious deeds, against each assault,
when he distributes alms to the destitute,
to those without means, and calls on the Lord,
455 the Father, for help; he hastens forth
from this fleeting life, stifles sins,
dark wicked deeds, maintains God's law
unafraid in his breast, turns to prayer
with pure thoughts, piously bows
460 his knee to earth, flees every evil,
dire sin, in dread of God.
Glad at heart he yearns to perform
the greatest number of good deeds; God
is his shield at all times, Lord of hosts,
465 Ruler of victories. These are the roots,
herbs, plants, that the wild bird culls
far and wide beneath the sky
for its dwelling-place, where it builds its nest
wondrously secure against all enmity.
470 Thus, the Lord's heroes accomplish His will
with might and main, in their habitations now,
attempt glorious deeds; the eternal Almighty
will grant them blessed guerdon for that.
From those herbs shall be fashioned a home for them
475 in the heavenly city, as meed for their deeds,
because they hotly cherished holy
precepts in their hearts. With surging souls
by day and night they love the Lord;
with fervent faith they choose the Beloved

43

480   ofer woruldwelan; ne biþ him wynne hyht
þæt hy þis læne lif long gewunien.
Þus eadig eorl ecan dreames,
heofona hames mid heahcyning
earnað on elne oþþæt ende cymeð
485   dogorrimes, þonne deað nimeð,
wiga wælgifre, wæpnum geþryþed,
ealdor anra gehwæs, ond in eorþan fæðm
snude sendað sawlum binumene
læne lichoman, þær hi longe beoð
490   oð fyres cyme foldan biþeahte.
Ðonne monge beoð on gemot lædaþ
fyra cynnes; wile fæder engla,
sigora soðcyning, seonoþ gehegan,
duguða dryhten, deman mid ryhte.
495   Þonne æriste ealle gefremmaþ
men on moldan, swa se mihtiga cyning
beodeð, brego engla, byman stefne
ofer sidne grund, sawla nergend.
Bið se deorca deað dryhtnes meahtum
500   eadgum geendad. Æðele hweorfað
þreatum þringað, þonne þeos woruld,
scyldwyrcende, in scome byrneð,
ade onæled. Weorþeð anra gehwylc
forht on ferþþe, þonne fyr briceð
505   læne londwelan, lig eal þigeð
eorðan æhtgestreon, æpplede gold
gifre forgripeð, grædig swelgeð
londes frætwe. Þonne on leoht cymeð
ældum þisses in þa openan tid
510   fæger ond gefealic fugles tacen,
þonne anwald eal up astellað
of byrgenum, ban gegrædað,
leomu lic somod, ond lifes gæst,
fore Cristes cneo. Cyning þrymlice
515   of his heahsetle halgum scineð,
wlitig wuldres gim. Wel biþ þam þe mot

480 above the world's wealth; not for them the hope
they will inhabit long this transitory life.
Thus may a blessed mortal bravely earn
eternal joy, a heavenly home,
with the high King, until an end comes
485 to his tally of days, when death,
the ravenous warrior, armed with weapons,
snatches the life of every man, and sends
frail bodies swiftly, bereft of souls,
into earth's embrace; where they will long
490 be covered by earth, till the fire's coming.
Then many of the race of men shall be led
into the assembly, and the Father of angels,
true King of victories, the Lord of hosts,
will hold a synod and judge with justice.
495 Then shall all men on earth achieve
resurrection, even as the mighty King,
Prince of angels, Saviour of souls, proclaims
His summons with trumpet blast across the wide world.
By the Lord's might, dark death shall be ended
500 for the blessed. Those noble beings shall go,
thronging in crowds, when this world,
working iniquity, burns in disgrace,
kindled with flame. Everyone shall feel
fearful in spirit, when fire destroys
505 the land's frail wealth and flame swallows all
earth's chattels, and eagerly grasps
dappled gold, and greedily devours
the world's wealth. Then, in that revealing time,
in radiance manifest to men shall be
510 gladsome, fair, this bird's betokening,
when the divine power shall raise up all
from their graves, and gather bones,
limbs and body, and spirit of life,
before Christ's knee. Gloriously the King,
515 from His high throne, shall shine on the holy,
a comely gem of glory. It will be well for those,

45

in þa geomran tid   gode lician.
Ðær þa lichoman,   leahtra clæne,
gongað glædmode,   gæstas hweorfað
520   in banfatu,   þonne bryne stigeð
heah to heofonum.   Hat bið monegum
egeslic æled,   þonne anra gehwylc,
soðfæst ge synnig,   sawel mid lice,
from moldgrafum   seceð meotudes dom,
525   forhtafæred.   Fyr bið on tihte,
æleð uncyste.   Þær þa eadgan beoð
æfter wræchwile   weorcum bifongen,
agnum dædum.   Þæt þa æþelan sind
wyrta wynsume,   mid þam se wilda fugel
530   his sylfes nest   biseteð utan,
þæt hit færinga   fyre byrneð,
forsweleð under sunnan,   ond he sylfa mid,
ond þonne æfter lige   lif eft onfehð
edniwinga.   Swa bið anra gehwylc
535   flæsce bifongen   fira cynnes,
ænlic ond edgeong,   se þe his agnum her
willum gewyrceð   þæt him wuldorcyning
meahtig æt þam mæþle   milde geweorþeð.
Þonne hleoþriað   halge gæstas,
540   sawla soðfæste,   song ahebbað,
clæne ond gecorene,   hergað cyninges þrym,
stefn æfter stefne,   stigað to wuldre
wlitige gewyrtad   mid hyra weldædum.
Beoð þonne amerede   monna gæstas,
545   beorhte abywde   þurh bryne fyres.
Ne wene þæs ænig   ælda cynnes
þæt ic lygewordum   leoð somnige —
write woðcræfte.   Gehyrað witedom
Iobes gieddinga.   Þurh gæstes blæd
550   breostum onbryded,   beald reordade,
wuldre geweorðad;   he þæt word gecwæð:
'Ic þæt ne forhycge   heortan geþoncum,
þæt ic in minum neste   neobed ceose,

who, in that dread hour, find favour with God.
Then will the bodies, cleansed of sins,
go glad-hearted, and souls return
520 to their frames, when the fire mounts
high to heaven. Hot for many
will that dread flame be, when every one,
righteous and sinful, soul with body,
from earthen graves shall seek God's doom,
525 aghast with fear; the fire shall advance,
burn wickedness. There the blessed will be
attired in their works, in their own deeds,
after their time in exile. These are the noble
and winsome herbs with which the wild bird
530 surrounds its own nest,
so that suddenly it burns with fire,
kindled under the sun, and itself with it,
and then, after the flame, its life again
renews. So every one of the race of men,
535 clothed in flesh, shall be unique
and young again, who, of his own will here,
brings it to pass that the mighty King,
will be merciful to him in that meeting.
Then holy spirits shall shout aloud,
540 righteous souls shall raise up song,
pure and elect, praise the King's majesty;
voice upon voice ascend to glory,
sweetly perfumed with their good deeds.
The souls of men shall then be cleansed,
545 brightly refined by the burning fire.
Let none of the race of men presume
that with lying words I compose my lay,
write my verse. Listen to the wisdom
of Job's songs. Through the spirit's gift,
550 stirred in his breast, gloriously honoured,
he boldly spoke and uttered these words:
'I do not scorn in my heart's thoughts,
to choose a death-bed in my nest,

hæle hrawerig,   gewite hean þonan
555 on longne sið,   lame bitolden,
geomor gudæda,   in greotes fæðm,
ond þonne æfter deaþe   þurh dryhtnes giefe
swa se fugel fenix   feorh edniwe
æfter æriste   agan mote,
560 dreamas mid dryhten,   þær seo deore scolu
leofne lofiað.   Ic þæs lifes ne mæg
æfre to ealdre   ende gebidan,
leohtes ond lissa.   Þeah min lic scyle
on moldærne   molsnad weorþan
565 wyrmum to willan,   swa þeah weoruda god
æfter swylthwile   sawle alyseð
ond in wuldor aweceð.   Me þæs wen næfre
forbirsteð in breostum,   ðe ic in brego engla
forðweardne gefean   fæste hæbbe.'
570   Ðus frod guma   on fyrndagum
gieddade gleawmod,   godes spelboda,
ymb his æriste   in ece lif,
þæt we þy geornor   ongietan meahten
tirfæst tacen   þæt se torhta fugel
575 þurh bryne beacnað.   Bana lafe,
ascan ond yslan,   ealle gesomnað
æfter ligbryne,   lædeþ siþþan
fugel on fotum   to frean geardum,
sunnan togeanes.   Þær hi siþþan forð
580 wuniað wintra fela,   wæstmum geniwad,
ealles edgiong,   þær ænig ne mæg
in þam leodscype   læþþum hwopan.
Swa nu æfter deaðe   þurh dryhtnes miht
somod siþiaþ   sawla mid lice,
585 fægre gefrætwed,   fugle gelicast,
in eadwelum   æþelum stencum,
þær seo soþfæste   sunne lihteð
wlitig ofer weoredum   in wuldres byrig.
        Ðonne soðfæstum   sawlum scineð
590 heah ofer hrofas   hælende Crist.

a man sore wearied, to go wretched thence
555   on the long journey, covered with clay,
in the dust's embrace, mourning my former deeds;
and then after death, by the grace of God,
after resurrection, just as the Phoenix bird,
I may be able to possess life anew,
560   pleasures with God, where the precious company
praise their Beloved. Of that life, I shall never
experience an ending to all eternity,
nor of its light, its loving joys. Though my corpse
shall decay in its earthen dwelling,
565   a delight to worms, yet the God of hosts
will set my soul free at the hour of death
and awaken it in glory. The hope of this
never fails in my breast, for I hold firm
to an abiding joy in the Prince of angels.'
570   Thus the wise man, discerning of mind,
God's spokesman, sang in distant days
of his resurrection into life everlasting,
that we might more clearly comprehend
the glorious significance that the bright bird
575   betokens by its burning. The remnants of bones,
ashes and cinders, it gathers all together
after the burning; then the bird brings
them in its claws to the Lord's abode,
towards the sun, where thenceforth they
580   remain for many years, renewed in form,
completely young again where none
in that land may threaten harm.
So now after death through the Lord's might,
souls together with body shall journey,
585   richly adorned, just like that bird,
with sweet perfume, into blessedness
where steadfastly true the sun shines radiant
above the hosts in the heavenly city.
Then on the righteous, high above its roofs,
590   the Saviour Christ will shine upon souls.

49

Him folgiað   fuglas scyne,
beorhte gebredade,   blissum hremige,
in þam gladan ham,   gæstas gecorene,
ece to ealdre.   Þær him yfle ne mæg
595   fah feond gemah   facne sceþþan,
ac þær lifgað a   leohte werede,
swa se fugel fenix,   in freoþu dryhtnes,
wlitige in wuldre.   Weorc anra gehwæs
beorhtne bliceð   in þam bliþam ham
600   fore onsyne   ecan dryhtnes,
symle in sibbe,   sunnan gelice.
Þær se beorhta beag,   brogden wundrum
eorcanstanum,   eadigra gehwam
hlifað ofer heafde.   Heafelan lixað,
605   þrymme biþeahte.   Ðeodnes cynegold
soðfæstra gehwone   sellic glengeð
leohte in life,   þær se longa gefea,
ece ond edgeong,   æfre ne sweþrað,
ac hy in wlite wuniað,   wuldre bitolden
610   fægrum frætwum,   mid fæder engla.
    Ne bið him on þam wicum   wiht to sorge,
wroht ne weþel   ne gewindagas,
hungor se hata   ne se hearde þurst,
yrmþu ne yldo.   Him se æþela cyning
615   forgifeð goda gehwylc.   Þær gæsta gedryht
hælend hergað   ond heofoncyninges
meahte mærsiað,   singað metude lof.
Swinsað sibgedryht   swega mæste
hædre ymb þæt halge   heahseld godes,
620   bliþe bletsiað   bregu selestan
eadge mid englum,   efenhleoþre þus:
'Sib si þe, soð god,   ond snyttrucræft,
ond þe þonc sy   þrymsittendum
geongra gyfena,   goda gehwylces.
625   Micel, unmæte   mægenes strenðu,
heah ond halig.   Heofonas sindon
fægre gefylled,   fæder ælmihtig,

Beautiful birds will follow him,
radiantly restored, gladly exulting
in that happy home, spirits elect
to all eternity. There the foul fiend
595 cannot basely hurt them by guile, but there
they shall live for ever, robed in light,
just like the Phoenix bird, in the Lord's peace,
beauteous in glory. Each one's achievement
will brightly shine in that blithe home
600 before the face of the eternal Lord,
perpetually in peace, like the sun.
There a bright halo, wondrously braided
with precious stones, will rise above the head
of each of the blessed; their brows will gleam,
605 crowned with majesty. A princely diadem
will gloriously adorn each righteous man
with light in that life, where lasting joy,
eternal and ever fresh, never wanes;
but they will dwell in beauty, gloriously clad
610 in fair adornments, with the Father of angels.
  No sorrow shall befall them in those abodes,
not strife, nor poverty, nor days of toil,
violent hunger nor cruel thirst,
disease nor age; the noble King will grant
615 them every good. There the company of souls
will praise the Saviour, and proclaim the might
of heaven's King, sing praises to the Lord.
The heavenly host will carol clearly,
in loudest harmony, around God's holy throne;
620 blithely the blessed together with the angels
will bless the best of Princes thus in unison:
'Peace be thine, true God, and wisdom's skill,
and thanks to thee, seated in majesty,
for thy fresh gifts, and for every good!
625 Great, immeasurable strength of might,
high and holy; the heavens are
fairly filled, Father almighty,

ealra þrymma þrym, þines wuldres,
uppe mid englum ond on eorðan somod.
630 Gefreoþa usic, frymþa scyppend. Þu eart fæder ælmihtig
in heannesse, heofuna waldend.'
Ðus reordiað ryhtfremmende,
manes amerede, in þære mæran byrig;
cyneþrym cyþað, caseres lof
635 singað on swegle soðfæstra gedryht,
þam anum is ece weorðmynd
forð butan ende. Næs his frymð æfre,
eades ongyn. Þeah he on eorþan her
þurh cildes had cenned wære
640 in middangeard hwæþre his meahta sped
heah ofer heofonum halig wunade,
dom unbryce. Þeah he deaþes cwealm
on rode treow ræfnan sceolde,
þearlic wite, he þy þriddan dæge
645 æfter lices hryre lif eft onfeng
þurh fæder fultum. Swa fenix beacnað,
geong in geardum, godbearnes meaht,
þonne he of ascan eft onwæcned
in lifes lif, leomum geþungen.
650 Swa se hælend us elpe gefremede
þurh his lices gedal, lif butan ende,
swa se fugel swetum his fiþru tu
ond wynsumum wyrtum gefylleð,
fægrum foldwæstmum, þonne afysed bið.
655 Þæt sindon þa word, swa us gewritu secgað,
hleoþor haligra, þe him to heofonum bið,
to þam mildan gode, mod afysed
in dreama dream, þær hi dryhtne to giefe
worda ond weorca wynsumne stenc
660 in þa mæran gesceaft meotude bringað,
in þæt leohte lif. Sy him lof symle
þurh woruld worulda, ond wuldres blæd,
ar ond onwald, in þam uplican
rodera rice. He is on ryht cyning

52

Majesty of all majesties, with thy glory
aloft with the angels, and also on earth.
630   Protect us, Lord of creation. Thou art the Father almighty,
Ruler of the heavens on high!'
Thus speak the righteous,
purged of guilt, in that glorious city;
the righteous band proclaim His royal majesty,
635   sing their Saviour's praise in heaven,
to whom alone is everlasting honour,
henceforth without end. His bliss had never
a beginning or inception, though here on earth He
was brought forth in the form of a child
640   into the world; yet the wealth of His powers
remained holy, high above the heavens,
glory inviolate. Though He was doomed
to suffer death's agony, terrible torment,
on the rood-tree, He on the third day
645   after His body's fall received life again
by the Father's help. Just so the Phoenix,
young in its dwelling, shows the might of God's Son,
when out of the ashes it wakes again
into the life of life, strong in its limbs.
650   Just as the Saviour afforded us aid,
life without end, through His body's death,
so this bird fills its two wings
with sweet and winsome herbs,
fair fruits of earth, when it is eager to be gone.
655   These are the words, the speech of saints,
—as Scripture tells us— whose spirits are urged
to be gone to heaven, to that gracious God,
to the joy of joys; where, as a gift to the Lord,
the Ordainer, they will bring the sweet scent
660   of words and works into that glorious realm,
into that radiant life. Praise be to Him for ever,
throughout all ages, and fullness of glory,
honour and power, in that celestial
kingdom of the skies. He is of right the King

53

665   middangeardes   ond mægenþrymmes,
             wuldre biwunden   in þære wlitigan byrig.
               Hafað us alyfed   *lucis auctor*
             þæt we motun her   *merueri,*
             goddædum begietan   *gaudia in celo,*
670   þær we motum   *maxima regna*
             secan ond gesittan   *sedibus altis,*
             lifgan in lisse   *lucis et pacis,*
             agan eardinga   *almæ letitie,*
             brucan blæddaga   *blandem et mittem*
675   geseon sigora frean   *sine fine,*
             ond him lof singan   *laude perenne,*
             eadge mid englum.   *Alleluia.*

665   of the world and of the heavenly hosts,
environed in glory in that fair city.
    He has allowed us, *Author of light*,
that here we may *merit*,
gain by good deeds, *delights in heaven*;
670   where we *extensive realms*
may seek and hold, *high seats*;
live in joy of *light and peace*;
have homes of *genial gladness*;
enjoy days of bliss, *gentle and mild*,
675   look on the Lord of victories, *without end*,
chant praise to Him, *perpetual praise*,
happy amid the angels. *Alleluia*.

The Panther

The Panther

Monge sindon   geond middangeard
unrimu cynn,   þe‚we æþelu ne magon
ryhte areccan   ne rim witan;
þæs wide sind   geond world innan
5   fugla ond deora   foldhrerendra
wornas widsceope,   swa wæter bibugeð
þisne beorhtan bosm   brim grymetende
sealtyþa geswing.   We bi sumum hyrdon
wrætlice gecynd   wildra secgan
10   firum freamærne   feorlondum on
eard weardian,   eðles neotan
æfter dunscrafum.   Is þæt deor pandher
bi noman haten,   þæs þe niþþa bearn,
wisfæste weras   on gewritum cyþað
15   bi þam anstapan.   Se is æghwam freond,
duguða estig,   butan dracan anum,
þam he in ealle tid   ondwrað leofaþ
þurh yfla gehwylc   þe he geæfnan mæg.
      Ðæt is wrætlic deor,   wundrum scyne
20   hiwa gehwylces;   swa hæleð secgað,
gæsthalge guman,   þætte Iosephes
tunece wære   telga gehwylces
bleom bregdende,   þara beorhtra gehwylc
æghwæs ænlicra   oþrum lixte
25   dryhta bearnum,   swa þæs deores hiw,
blæc brigda gehwæs,   beorhtra ond scynra
wundrum lixeð,   þætte wrætlicra
æghwylc oþrum,   ænlicra gien
ond fægerra   frætwum bliceð,
30   symle sellicra.   He hafað sundorgecynd,
milde, gemetfæst.   He is monþwære,
lufsum ond leoftæl,   nele laþes wiht
ængum geæfnan   butan þam attorsceaþan,
his fyrngeflitan,   þe ic ær fore sægde.
35   Symle fylle fægen,   þonne foddor þigeð,

The Panther

Throughout middle-earth there are many
kinds of creatures, whose nature we cannot
rightly recount or know the number;
so widely scattered throughout the world
5   are the multitudes of birds and beasts
that move on the earth, even as water,
the roaring sea, the salt waves' swell,
girds this bright bosom. We have heard tell
of the wondrous nature of one wild beast
10   that, in a far land famous among men,
bides in a dwelling, holds his domain,
amid mountain caves. That beast is called
Panther by name, as the sons of men,
men of wisdom, have told us in writings
15   about that lone-stepper. He is a friend to all,
gracious in gifts, save only the serpent,
with whom he always lives in hostility
for every evil which he can effect.
       That is a beauteous beast wondrously radiant
20   in all his hues; just as heroes,
men holy in spirit, say that Joseph's
coat shimmered in colours
of every dye, each of which, brighter
and more splendid than the other, shone
25   among the sons of men, so this beast's hue,
brighter and more brilliant in its variety,
shines wondrously, so that each was more
marvellous than the others, yet more unique
and fairer in its beauty,
30   always much rarer. He has a strange nature,
mild, slow to wrath. He is gentle,
loving, and kind; he will do no harm
to anyone save that venomous foe,
his old enemy, of whom I spoke before.
35   Ever pleased with plenty, when he consumes food,

59

æfter þam gereordum   ræste seceð
dygle stowe   under dunscrafum;
ðær se þeodwiga   þreonihta fæc
swifeð on swefote   slæpe gebiesgad.
40   Þonne ellenrof   up astondeð,
þrymme gewelgad,   on þone þriddan dæg,
sneome of slæpe.   Sweghleoþor cymeð,
wopa wynsumast   þurh þæs wildres muð.
Æfter þære stefne   stenc ut cymeð
45   of þam wongstede,   wynsumra steam,
swettra ond swiþra   swæcca gehwylcum,
wyrta blostmum   ond wudubledum,
eallum æþelicra   eorþan frætwum.
Þonne of ceastrum   ond cynestolum
50   ond of burgsalum   beornþreat monig
farað foldwegum   folca þryþum,
eoredcystum,   ofestum gefysde,
dareðlacende;   deor efne swa some
æfter þære stefne   on þone stenc farað.
55   Swa is dryhten god,   dreama rædend,
eallum eaðmede   oþrum gesceaftum,
duguða gehwylcre,   butan dracan anum,
attres ordfruman.   Þæt is se ealda feond,
þone he gesælde   in susla grund,
60   ond gefetrade   fyrnum teagum,
biþeahte þreanydum,   ond þy þriddan dæge
of digle aras,   þæs þe he deað fore us
þreoniht þolade,   þeoden engla,
sigora sellend.   Þæt wæs swete stenc,
65   wlitig ond wynsum   geond woruld ealle.
Siþþan to þam swicce   soðfæste men
on healfa gehwone   heapum þrungon
geond ealne ymbhwyrft   eorþan sceata.
Swa se snotra gecwæð   sanctus Paulus:
70   'Monigfealde sind   geond middangeard
god ungnyðe   þe us to giefe dæleð
ond to feorhnere   fæder ælmihtig,

60

he seeks rest after feasting,
a secret spot in the mountain-caves;
there, for three nights, the great warrior
drowses in slumber, sunk in sleep.
40 Then, valiant, enriched with strength,
on the third day he rises up
swiftly from sleep. A melody comes forth,
sweetest of songs, from the beast's mouth.
After that voice an odour issues
45 from the place, a breath more pleasant,
sweeter and stronger than all the scents
of flowering herbs and forest fruits,
more excellent than all the treasures of earth.
Then from cities and royal seats
50 and castle-halls many crowds of men,
troops of men, traverse earth-tracks,
javelin-throwers in troops
impelled by haste; animals, too,
after the voice, are drawn to the smell.
55 Thus is the Lord God, Giver of joys,
gracious of every gift to all
other creatures save only the serpent,
the author of venom. That is the ancient fiend
whom He bound in the abyss of torments,
60 and fettered with fiery chains,
loaded with misery; and, on the third day, He
rose from His secret spot, Prince of angels,
Giver of victories, after He suffered death
for us three nights. That was a sweet smell,
65 fair and winsome, throughout the whole world.
Later pious men to that perfume
hastened in hosts on every hand
over all the extent of the regions of earth.
Thus spoke St Paul in his wisdom:
70 'Manifold and generous throughout the world
are the good things granted us as a gift
to save our lives by the Father Almighty,

61

ond se anga hyht   ealra gesceafta,
uppe ge niþre.'   Þæt is æþele stenc.

the only Hope of all created beings
above and below.' That is an excellent smell.

The Whale

The Whale

Nu ic fitte gen   ymb fisca cynn
wille woðcræfte   wordum cyþan
þurh modgemynd   bi þam miclan hwale.
Se bið unwillum   oft gemeted,
5   frecne ond ferðgrim,   fareðlacendum,
niþþa gehwylcum;   þam is noma cenned,
fyrnstreama geflotan,   Fastitocalon.
Is þæs hiw gelic   hreofum stane,
swylce worie   bi wædes ofre,
10   sondbeorgum ymbseald,   særyrica mæst,
swa þæt wenaþ   wægliþende
þæt hy on ealond sum   eagum wliten,
ond þonne gehydað   heahstefn scipu
to þam unlonde   oncyrrapum,
15   sælaþ sæmearas   sundes æt ende,
ond þonne in þæt eglond   up gewitað
collenferþe;   ceolas stondað
bi staþe fæste,   streame biwunden.
Ðonne gewiciað   werigferðe,
20   faroðlacende,   frecnes ne wenað,
on þam ealonde   æled weccað,
heahfyr ælað;   hæleþ beoþ on wynnum,
reonigmode,   ræste geliste.
Þonne gefeleð   facnes cræftig
25   þæt him þa ferend on   fæste wuniaþ,
wic weardiað   wedres on luste,
ðonne semninga   on sealtne wæg
mid þa noþe   niþer gewiteþ
garsecges gæst,   grund geseceð,
30   ond þonne in deaðsele   drence bifæsteð
scipu mid scealcum.   Swa biþ scinna þeaw,
deofla wise,   þæt hi drohtende
þurh dyrne meaht   duguðe beswicað,
ond on teosu tyhtaþ   tilra dæda,
35   wemað on willan,   þæt hy wraþe secen,

66

The Whale

Now a fitt about a kind of fish
I will frame by my wit, a song
with words about the mighty whale.
   To their sorrow he is often found
5   by seafarers, fierce and cruel
to every man; this name is given
to the ocean-floater: *Fastitocalon.*
His shape is like a rough stone,
as if great sea-weeds, girt
10   by sandbanks, floated by the shore,
so that seafarers suppose
their eyes behold an isle;
and then secure their high-prowed ships
by anchor-ropes to that false land;
15   stall their sea-steeds at the water's edge,
and then go up into that isle,
stout-hearted; their ships stand
fast by the shore, engirt by streams.
Then the weary mariners
20   encamp, expecting no harm;
on that isle, they kindle fire,
build a great blaze; the men,
worn out, gladly long for rest.
When he, skilled in treachery, feels
25   the sailors settled firm upon him,
encamped, enjoying the clear weather,
then suddenly the ocean-spirit
dives down with his prey
into the salt wave, seeks the depths,
30   and in the death-hall tries to drown
ships and crews. Such is the wont of demons,
the way of devils, that, living, they
betray men through dark might,
draw them to ruin of their good deeds,
35   entice them to pleasure; so that they seek

67

frofre to feondum,   oþþæt hy fæste ðær
æt þam wærlogan   wic geceosað.
Þonne þæt gecnaweð   of cwicsusle
flah feond gemah, ˛ þætte fira gehwylc
40   hæleþa cynnes   on his hringe biþ
fæste gefeged,   he him feorgbona
þurh sliþen searo   siþþan weorþeð,
wloncum ond heanum,   þe his willan her
firenum fremmað;   mid þam he færinga,
45   heoloþhelme biþeaht,   helle seceð,
goda geasne,   grundleasne wylm
under mistglome,   swa se micla hwæl,
se þe bisenceð   sæliþende
eorlas ond yðmearas.   He hafað oþre gecynd,
50   wæterþisa wlonc,   wrætlicran gien.
Þonne hine on holme   hungor bysgað
ond þone aglæcan   ætes lysteþ,
ðonne se mereweard   muð ontyneð,
wide weleras;   cymeð wynsum stenc
55   of his innoþe,   þætte oþre þurh þone,
sæfisca cynn,   beswicen weorðaþ,
swimmað sundhwate   þær se sweta stenc
ut gewitað.   Hi þær in farað
unware weorude,   oþþæt se wida ceafl
60   gefylled bið;   þonne færinga
ymbe þa herehuþe   hlemmeð togædre
grimme goman.   Swa bið gumena gehwam,
se þe oftost his   unwærlice
on þas lænan tid   lif bisceawað,
65   læteð hine beswican   þurh swetne stenc,
leasne willan,   þæt he biþ leahtrum fah
wið wuldorcyning.   Him se awyrgda ongean
æfter hinsiþe   helle ontyneð,
þam þe leaslice   lices wynne
70   ofer ferhðgereaht   fremedon on unræd.
Þonne se fæcna   in þam fæstenne
gebroht hafað,   bealwes cræftig,

68

solace from foes, till they firmly choose
a dwelling with the devil there.
When from his hell-torment the false
impious fiend knows that any one
40   of the human race is firmly fixed
on his round form, he then becomes
the slayer by artful sleights,
of high and low, who, in wickedness,
work his will here; with these he quickly,
45   helmet-hidden, void of virtue,
seeks hell, the bottomless surge,
under misty gloom, even as the mighty whale
who sinks seafaring
men and ships. Bold water-rusher, he
50   has yet another wondrous trait.
When hunger harries him on the wave
and the creature craves for food,
then the sea-warden opens his mouth,
his wide lips; a winsome smell comes
55   from within him so that other kinds
of fish are thereby deceived.
They swim swiftly to where the sweet smell
issues forth. They enter there
in a thoughtless throng, till the wide jaw
60   is filled; then suddenly
he crashes his fierce jaws together
about the plunder. So it is for every man
who most often heedlessly
considers life in this lean time;
65   he lets himself be snared by a sweet smell,
a false desire, so that he is stained with sins
against the King of glory. The accursed one
opens hell to him after his journey hence,
and, to those who, falsely and foolishly, follow
70   the joys of flesh against the advice of the soul.
When the deceiver, cunning in evil,
has brought into that fastness,

æt þam edwylme   þa þe him on cleofiað,
gyltum gehrodene,   ond ær georne his
75   in hira lifdagum   larum hyrdon,
þonne he þa grimman   goman bihlemmeð
æfter feorhcwale ᵗfæste togædre,
helle hlinduru;   nagon hwyrft ne swice,
utsiþ æfre,   þa þær in cumað,
80   þon ma þe þa fiscas   faraðlacende
of þæs hwæles fenge   hweorfan motan.
Forþon is eallinga   * * *
dryhtna dryhtne,   ond a deoflum wiðsace
wordum ond weorcum,   þæt we wuldorcyning
85   geseon moton.   Uton a sibbe to him
on þas hwilnan tid   hælu secan,
þæt we mid swa leofne   in lofe motan
to widan feore   wuldres neotan.

that fiery lake, those who, loaded with sins,
called to him, and who once eagerly
75   listened to his counsels in their life-days,
then, after the carnage, he clashes
fast together those fierce jaws,
hell's prison doors; nor freedom, nor escape,
nor egress ever, have they who enter there,
80   any more than those fishes, swimmers in the sea,
may return from the whale's grasp.
Wherefore, it is wholly (best for us to please)
the Lord of lords and ever fight fiends
by words and deeds, that we may see
85   the King of glory. Let us ever seek from Him
grace and salvation in this short time,
that we may savour heaven for ever
in glory with One so beloved.

The Partridge

The Partridge

Hyrde ic secgan gen   bi sumum fugle
wundorlice * * *

The Partridge

Next I have heard tell a wonderful ....
about a certain bird ....

Notes

1   C L Wrenn, *A Study of Old English Literature* (London, 1970), p.129.

2   R K Gordon, *Anglo-Saxon Poetry* (London, 1962), p.239.

3   C W Kennedy, *An Anthology of Old English Poetry* (New York, 1960), p.97.

4   C W Kennedy, *Early English Christian Poetry* (New York, 1963), p.217.

5   L J Rodrigues, *Anglo-Saxon Didactic Verse* (Llanerch, 1995), p.27.

6   See **Appendix 1** (i).

7   In two late-eleventh century manuscripts, British Museum Cotton Vespasian D xiv, fol. 166r-168r, and Cambridge, Corpus Christi College 198, fol. 374b-377a, the allegory in this detail is definitely clarified and sharpened. These late versions state that the Earthly Paradise contained the *fons vitae*, or fountain of life, in which the Phoenix bathed. See **Appendix 1** (iii) for the Vespasian version.

8   A S Cook, *The Old English Elene, Phoenix, and Physiologus* (New Haven, 1919), p.115.

9   *Phoenix*, 335-60.

10   That the poet intended the flocks of birds as symbols of the hosts of righteous souls who accompany their risen Lord is explicit in lines 591-4 of the *Phoenix*.

11   *Phoenix*, 552-69.

12   Job xix 25-6.

13   Cook, op.cit., pp. lxxxi-lxxxv.

14   For Milton's use of the story, see *Paradise Lost*, I 200-8.

Abbreviations

Archiv	*Archiv für das Studium der neuren Sprachen und Literaturen*
EETS o.s.	Early English Text Soxiety, old series
JEGP	*Journal of English and Germanic Philology*
MLN	*Modern Language Notes*
MLQ	*Modern Language Quarterly*
MPh	*Modern Philology*
Neophil	*Neophilologus*
NM	*Neuphilologische Mitteilungen*
N&Q	*Notes and Queries*
OE	Old English
UCPCP	*University of California Publications in Classical Philology*

Select Bibliography

1. Editions

Blake, N F, ed.: *The Phoenix* (Manchester, 1964); revd. (Exeter, 1990).

Chambers, R W, Förster M and Flower R, eds.: *The Exeter Book of Old English Poetry*, facsimile edition (London 1933).

Cook, A S, ed.: *The Old English Elene, Phoenix and Physiologus* (New Haven and London, 1919).

Gollanz, I, ed.: *The Exeter Book, Part I*: Poems i-viii, EETS o.s. 104 (London, 1895).

Grein C W M, ed.: *Bibliothek der Angelsächsischen Poesie*, 4 vols. (Göttingen,1857-64); revd., Wülker, R P, 3 vols. (Leipzig, 1881-97).

Krapp G P and Dobbie, E van K, eds.: *The Exeter Book*, vol. III, The Anglo-Saxon Poetic Records (London and New York, 1936).

Mackie, W S, ed.: *The Exeter Book, Part. II*: Poems ix-xxxii, EETS o.s. 194 (Oxford, 1934) [with facing translation].

Muir, B J, ed.: *The Exeter Anthology of Old English Poetry*, 2 vols. (Exeter, 1994).

Squires, A, ed.: *The Old English Physiologus* (Durham, 1988).

Thorpe, B, ed.: *Codex Exoniensis* (London, 1842).

2. Translations

Bradley, S A J: *Anglo-Saxon Poetry* (London, 1982).

Cook, A S and Tinker, C B: *Select Translations from Old English Poetry*. Revd. edn. (Harvard, 1935).

Faust C and Thomson, S: *Old English Poems, Translated into the Original Meter* (Chicago, 1918).

Gordon, R K: *Anglo-Saxon Poetry*. Revd. edn. (London, 1954).

Hall, J L: *Judith, Phoenix, and other Anglo-Saxon Poems* (New York, 1902).

Hamer, R F S: *A Choice of Anglo-Saxon Verse* (London, 1970).

Kennedy, C W: *The Poems of Cynewulf Translated into English Prose* (London, 1910).

———: *Early English Christian Poetry Translated into Alliterative*

Verse (London, 1952).

———: *An Anthology of Old English Poetry Translated into Alliterative Verse* (New York, 1960) [*The Phoenix* 1-392].

3. Critical Studies

(a) General

Alexander M: *Old English Literature* (London, 1983).

Calder, D G, Bjork, R E, Ford P K, and Mella DF: *Sources and Analogues of Old English Poetry*, 2 vols. (Cambridge, 1977-83).

Campbell, J J: 'Learned Rhetoric in Old English Poetry', *MPh* lxiii (1966), 189-201.

———: 'Knowledge of Rhetorical Figures in Anglo-Saxon England', *JEGP* lxvi (1967), 1-20.

Cavill, P: 'Sectional Divisions in Old English Poetic Manuscripts', *Neophil* lxix (1985), 156-9.

Conner, P W: *A Contextual Study of the Old English Exeter Book* (University of Maryland dissertation, 1975).

Gardiner, J: *The Construction of Christian Poetry in Old English* (Carbondale, 1975).

Gatch, M Mc: *Death: Meaning and Mortality in Christian Thought and Contemporary Culture* (New York, 1969).

Greenfield, S B: *A Critical History of Old English Literature* (New York, 1965).

———: *The Interpretation of Old English Poems* (London, 1972).

——— and Calder, D G: *A New Critical History of Old English Literature* (New York, 1986).

Isaacs N D: *Structural Principles in Old English Poetry* (Knoxville, 1968).

Opland, J: *Anglo-Saxon Oral Poetry: A Study of Tradition* (New Haven, 1980).

Raw, B C: *The Art and Background of Old English Poetry* (London, 1978).

Shippey, T A: *Old English Verse* (London, 1972).

Stanley, E G: 'Studies in the Prosaic Vocabulary of Old English Verse', *NM*, lxxii (1971), 385-418.

Swanton, M J: *English Literature before Chaucer* (London, 1987).

Wilson J H: *Christian Theology and Old English Poetry* (The Hague, 1974).
Wrenn, C L: *A Study of Old English Literature* (London, 1967).

(b) *Poems*
The Phoenix
Blake, N F: 'Originality in "The Phoenix"', *N&Q* ccvi (1961), 326-7.
———: 'Some problems of Interpretation and Translation in the OE *Phoenix*', *Anglia* lxxx (1962), 50-62.
Fulton, E: 'On the Authorship of the Anglo-Saxon Poem Phoenix', *MLN* xi (1896), 146-69.
Klaeber, F: 'Emendations in Old Englsih Poems', *MPh* ii (1904-5), 141-6.
Shearin, H G: 'The *Phoenix* and the *Guthlac*', *MLN* xxii (1907), 263.

The Physiologus
Campbell, T P: 'Thematic Unity in the Old English *Physiologus*', *Archiv* ccxv (1978), 73-9.
Cook, A S: 'The Old English *Whale*', *MLN* ix (1894), 65-8.
Cordasco, F: 'The Old English Physiologus: Its Problems', *MLQ* x (1949), 351-5.
Ebert, A: 'Der angelsachsische *Physiologus*', *Anglia* vi (1883), 241-7.
Letson, D R: 'The Old English *Physiologus* and the Homiletic Tradition', *Florilegium* i (1979), 15-41.
Peebles, R J: 'The Anglo-Saxon *Physiologus*', *MPh* viii (1910-11), 571-9.
Pitman, J H: 'Milton and the *Physiologus*', *MLN* xl (1925), 439-40.

4. *Sources*

(a) *The Phoenix*
Baehrens, A: *Poetae Latini Minores*, vol.iii (Leipzig, 1881).
Duff, J W and A M: *Minor Latin Poems*, 2nd edn. (London and Cambridge, Mass., 1954).

81

Fitzpatrick, M C: *Lactanti de ave phoenice* (University of Philadelphia dissertation, 1933).

Richmond, O L: *De ave phoenice* (Edinburgh, 1947).

Riese, A: *Anthologia Latina pars prima*, vol.ii, 2nd edn. (Leipzig, 1906).

(b) *The Physiologus*

Ahrens, K: *Zur Geschichte des sogenannten Physiologus* (Ploen, 1885).

Carmody, F J, ed.: *Physiologus Latinus: Editions préliminaires versio B* (Paris, 1939).

——: 'Physiologus Latinus Versio Y', *UCPCP* xii (1933-44), 96-134.

Lauchert, F: *Geschichte des Physiologus* (Strassburg, 1889).

Sbordone, F: *Richerche sulle fonti e sulla composizione del Physiologus greco* (Naples, 1936).

Appendices

Appendix 1
(i) Lactantius' *Carmen de ave phoenice*
[based on H W Garrod's *The Oxford Book of Latin Verse* (1912), pp. 362-7]

Est locus in primo felix oriente remotus,
  qua patet aeterni maxima porta poli.
nec tamen aestiuos hiemisue propinquus ad ortus
  sed qua sol uerno fundit ab axe diem.
5   illic planities tractus diffundit apertos,
  nec tumulus crescit nec caua uallis hiat,
sed nostros montis, quorum iuga celsa putantur,
  per bis sex ulnas imminet ille locus.
hic Solis nemus est et consitus arbore multa
10   lucus, perpetuae frondis honore uirens.
cum Phaethonteis flagrasset ab ignibus axis,
  ille locus flammis inuiolatus erat;
et cum diluuium mersisset fluctibus orbem
  Deucalioneas exsuperauit aquas.
15   non huc exsangues Morbi, non aegra Senectus,
  nec Mors crudelis nec Metus asper adest,
nec Scelus infandum nec opum uesana Cupido
  aut Sitis aut ardens caedis amore Furor;
Luctus acerbus abest et Egestas obsita pannis
20   et Curae insomnes et uiolenta Fames.
non ibi tempestas nec uis furit horrida uenti
  nec gelido terram rore pruina tegit,
nulla super campos tendit sua uellera nubes
  nec cadit ex alto turbidus umor aquae.
25   est fons in medio, quem 'uiuum' nomine dicunt,
  perspicuus, lenis, dulcibus uber aquis;
qui semel erumpens per singula tempora mensum
  duodecies undus inrigat omne nemus.
hic genus arboreum procero stipite surgens
30   non lapsura solo mitia poma gerit.
hoc nemus, hos lucos auis incolit unica Phoenix,
  unica si uiuit morte refecta sua.

84

There is a far-off land, blest amid the first streaks of dawn, where the mightiest portal of the everlasting sky stands open, yet not beside the risings of the summer or the winter Sun, but where he sheds daylight from the heavens in spring. There is a plain spreads out its open levels; no knoll swells there, no hollow valley gapes, yet that region is higher by twice six ells than our mountains whose ridges are considered high. Here is the grove of the Sun — a woodland planted with many a tree and green with the honours of eternal foliage. When the sky went ablaze from the fires of Phaethon's car, that region was inviolate from the flames; it rose above the waters on which Deucalion sailed, when the flood had whelmed the world in its waves. Hither no bloodless diseases come, no sickly age, nor cruel death nor desperate fear nor nameless crime nor maddened lust for wealth or wrath or frenzy afire with the love of murder; bitter grief is absent and beggary beset with rags and sleepless cares and violent hunger. No tempest raves there nor savage force of wind: nor does the hoar-frost shroud the ground in chill damp. Above the plains no cloud stretches its fleece, nor falls from on high the stormy moisture of rain. But there is a well in the midst, the well of life they call it, crystal-clear, gently-flowing, rich in its sweet waters: bursting forth once for each several month in its season, it drenches all the grove twelve times with its flood. Here is a kind of tree that rising with stately stem bears mellow fruits which will not fall to the ground.

In this grove, in these woods, dwells the peerless bird, the Phoenix, peerless, since she lives renewed by her own death. An

85

paret et obsequitur Phoebo ueneranda satelles:
hoc Natura parens munus habere dedit.
35 lutea cum primum surgens Aurora rubescit,
cum primum rosea sidera luce fugat,
ter quater illa pias inmergit corpus in undas,
ter quater e uiuo gurgite libat aquam.
tollitur ac summo considit in arboris altae
40 uertice, quae totum despicit una nemus,
et conuersa nouos Phoebi nascentis ad ortus
exspectat radios et iubar exoriens.
atque ubi Sol pepulit fulgentis limina portae
et primi emicuit luminis aura leuis,
45 incipit illa sacri modulamina fundere cantus
et mira lucem uoce ciere nouam;
quam nec aëdoniae uoces nec tibia possit
musica Cirrhaeis adsimulare modis,
et neque olor moriens imitari posse putetur
50 nec Cylleneae fila canora lyrae.
postquam Phoebus equos in aperta effudit Olympi
atque orbem totum protulit usque means,
illa ter alarum repetito uerbere plaudit
igniferumque caput ter uenerata silet.
55 atque eadem celeris etiam discriminat horas
innarrabilibus nocte dieque sonis,
antistes luci nemorumque uerenda sacerdos
et sola arcanis conscia, Phoebe, tuis.
quae postquam uitae iam mille peregerit annos
60 ac si reddiderint tempora longa grauem,
ut reparet lapsum spatiis uergentibus aeuum,
adsuetum nemoris dulce cubile fugit;
cumque renascendi studio loca sancta reliquit,
tunc petit hunc orbem, mors ubi regna tenet.
65 derigit in Syriam celeris longaeua uolatus,
Phoenicen nomen cui dedit ipsa uetus,
secretosque petit deserta per auia lucos,
sicubi per saltus silua remota latet.
tum legit aërio sublimem uertice palmam,

86

acolyte worthy of record, she yields obedience and homage to Phoebus: such the duty that parent Nature assigned to her for observance. Soon as saffron Aurora reddens at her rising, soon as she routs the stars with rosy light, thrice and again that bird plunges her body into the kindly waves, thrice and again sips water from the living flood. Soaring she settles on the topmost height of a lofty tree which alone commands the whole of the grove, and, turning towards the fresh rising of Phoebus at his birth, awaits the emergence of his radiant beam. And when the Sun has struck the threshold of the gleaming portal and the light shaft of his first radiance has flashed out, she begins to pour forth notes of hallowed minstrelsy and to summon the new day in a marvellous key which neither tune of nightingale nor musical pipe could rival in Cirrhean modes; nay, let not the dying swan be thought capable of imitating it, nor yet the tuneful strings of Cyllenean lyre.

After Phoebus has given his steeds the rein into the open heavens and in ever onward course brought forth his full round orb, then that bird with thrice repeated beat of the wing yields her applause, and after three obeisances to the fire-bearing prince holds her peace. She it is also who marks off the swift hours by day and night in sounds which may not be described, priestess of the grove and awe-inspiring ministrant of the woods, the only confidant of thy mysteries, Phoebus. When she has already fulfilled a thousand years of life and long lapse of time has made it burdensome to her, she flees from her sweet and wonted nest in the grove, so that in the closing span she may restore her bygone existence, and when in passion for rebirth she has left her sacred haunts, then she seeks this world where death holds sovereignty. Despite her length of years she directs her swift flight into Syria, to which she herself of old gave the name of 'Phoenice', and seeks through desert wilds the care-free groves, here where the sequestered woodland lurks among the glades. Then she chooses a palm-tree towering with airy crest

70   quae Graium Phoenix ex aue nomen habet,
in quam nulla nocens animans prorepere possit,
lubricus aut serpens aut auis ulla rapax.
tum uentos claudit pendentibus Aeolus antris,
ne uiolent flabris aëra purpureum,
75   neu concreta noto nubes per inania caeli
submoueat radios solis et obsit aui.
construit inde sibi seu nidum siue sepulcrum:
nam perit ut uiuat, se tamen ipsa creat.
colligit hinc sucos et odores diuite silua,
80   quos legit Assyrius, quos opulentus Araps,
quos aut Pygmaeae gentes aut India carpit
aut molli generat terra Sabaea sinu.
cinnamon hic auramque procul spirantis amomi
congerit et mixto balsama cum polio.
85   non casiae mitis nec olens suffimen acanthi
nec turis lacrimae guttaque pinguis abest.
his addit teneras nardi pubentis aristas
et sociat myrrae uim, Nabathaea, tuae.
protinus instructo corpus mutabile nido
90   uitalique toro membra uieta locat.
ore dehinc sucos membris circumque supraque
inicit exsequiis immoritura suis. .
tunc inter uarios animam commendat odores,
depositi tanti nec timet illa fidem.
95   interea corpus genitali morte peremptum
aestuat, et flammam parturit ipse calor,
aetherioque procul de lumine concipit ignem,
flagrat et ambustum soluitur in cineres.
quos uelut in massam generans in morte coactos
100   conflat; et effectum seminis instar habet.
complerit mensum si fetus tempora certa,
sese oui teretis colligit in speciem;
hinc animal primum sine membris fertur oriri,
sed fertur uermi lacteus esse color:
105   ac uelut agrestes, cum filo ad saxa tenentur,
mutari tineae papilione solent.

88

which bears its Greek name 'Phoenix' from the bird: against it no hurtful living creature could steal forth, or slippery serpent, or any bird of prey. Then Aeolus imprisons the winds in over-arching grottoes, lest their blasts harass the bright-gleaming air, or the cloud-wrack from the South banish the rays of sun throughout the empty tracts of heaven and do harm to the bird. Thereafter she builds herself a cradle or sepulchre — which you will — for she dies to live and yet begets herself. She gathers for it from the rich forest juicy scented herbs such as the Assyrian gathers or the wealthy Arabian, such as either the Pgymaean races or India culls or the Sabaean land produces in its soft bosom. Here she heaps together cinnamon and effluence of the aromatic shrub that sends its breath afar and balsam with its blended leaf. Nor is there lacking a slip of mild cassia or fragrant acanthus or the rich dropping tears of frankincense. Thereto she adds the tender ears of downy spikenard, joining as its ally the potency of thy myrrh, Panachaea. Forthwith in the nest she has furnished she sets her body that awaits its change — withered limbs on a life-giving couch: thereafter with her beak she casts the scents on her limbs, around them and above, being appointed to die in her own funeral. Then she commends her soul amid the varied fragrances without a fear for the trustworthiness of a deposit so great. Meanwhile her body, destroyed by birth-giving, is aglow, the very heat producing flame and catching fire from the ethereal light afar: it blazes and when burned dissolves into ashes. She welds these ashes together, as if they were concentrated by moisture in a mass, possessing in the result what takes the place of seed. Therefrom, it is said, rises a living creature first of all without limbs, but this worm is said to have a milky colour: when suddenly at the appointed hour it has grown enormously, gathering into what looks like a rounded egg, from it she is remoulded in such shape as she had before, bursting her shell and springing to life a Phoenix:

inde reformatur quali fuit ante figura
et Phoenix ruptis pullulat exuuiis.
non illi cibus est nostro concessus in orbe
110   nec cuiquam inplumem pascere cura subest;
ambrosios libat caelesti nectare rores,
stellifero tenues qui cecidere polo.
hos legit, his alitur mediis in odoribus ales,
donec maturam proferat effigiem.
115   ast ubi primaeua coepit florere iuuenta,
euolat ad patrias iam reditura domus.
ante tamen, proprio quicquid de corpore restat,
ossaque uel cineres exuuiasque suas
unguine balsameo myrraque et ture soluto
120   condit et in formam conglobat ore pio.
quam pedibus gestans contendit Solis ad urbem
inque ara residens ponit in aede sacra.
mirandam sese praestat praebetque uerendam:
tantus aui decor est, tantus abundat honor.
125   praecipuus color est, quali sunt sidera caeli,
praecoqua uel qualis Punica grana tegit:
qualis inest foliis, quae fert agreste papauer,
cum pandit uestes Flora rubente solo.
hoc humeri pectusque decens uelamine fulgent,
130   hoc caput, hoc ceruix summaque terga nitent;
caudaque porrigitur fuluo distincta metallo,
in cuius maculis purpura mixta rubet;
aura auri pennas insignit, desuper Iris
pingere ceu nubis splendida rore solet;
135   albicat insignis mixto uiridante smaragdo
et puro cornu gemmea cuspis hiat:
ingentes oculos credas geminos hyacinthos
quorum de medio lucida flamma micat;
arquata est rutilo capiti radiata corona
140   Phoebei referens uerticis alta decus;
crura tegunt squamae Tyrio depicta ueneno,
ast unguis roseo tinguit honore color.
effigies inter pauonis mixta figuram

it is even so that larvae in the country fastened by threads to stones are wont to change into a butterfly. Hers is no food familiar in this world of ours: it is no one's charge to feed the bird as yet unfledged: she sips ambrosial dews of heavenly nectar fallen in a fine shower from the star-bearing sky. Such is her culling, such her sustenance, encompassed by fragrant spices until she bring her appearance to maturity. But when she begins to bloom in the spring-time of her youth, she flits forth already bent on a return to her ancestral abodes. Yet ere she goes, she takes all that remains of what was her own body — bones or ashes and the shell that was hers — and stores it in balsam oil, myrrh, and frankincense set free, rounding it into ball-shape with loving beak. Bearing this in her talons she speeds to the City of the Sun, and perching on the altar sets it in the hallowed temple. Marvellous is her appearance and the show she makes to the onlooker: such comeliness has the bird, so ample a glory. To begin with, her colour is like the colour which beneath the sunshine of the sky ripe pomegranates cover under their rind; like the colour in the petals of the wild poppy when Flora displays her garb at the blush of dawn. In such dress gleam her shoulders and comely breast; even so glitter head and neck and surface of the back, while the tail spreads out variegated with a metallic yellow, amid whose spots reddens a purple blend. The wing-feathers are picked out by a contrasted sheen, as it is the heaven-sent rainbow's way to illuminate the clouds. The beak is of a fine white with a dash of emerald green, glittering like a jewel in its clear horn as it opens. You would take for twin sapphires those great eyes from between which shoots a bright flame. All over the head is fitted a crown of rays, in lofty likeness to the glory of the Sun-god's head. Scales cover the legs, which are variegated with a metallic yellow, but the tint which colours the claws is a wonderful rose. To the eye it has a blended semblance between the peacock's

cernitur et pictam Phasidis inter auem.
145 magnitiem, terris Arabum quae gignitur, ales
uix aequare potest, seu fera seu sit auis.
non tamen est tarda, ut uolucres quae corpore magno
incessus pigros per graue pondus habent,
sed leuis ac uelox, regali plena decore;
150 talis in aspectu se tenet usque hominum.
huc uenit Aegyptus tanti ad miracula uisus
et raram uolucrem turba salutat ouans.
protinus exsculpunt sacrato in marmore formam
et titulo signant remque diemque nouo.
155 contrahit in coetum sese genus omne uolantum,
nec praedae memor est ulla nec ulla metus.
alituum stipata choro uolat illa per altum
turbaque prosequitur munere laeta pio.
sed postquam puri peruenit ad aetheris auras,
160 mox redit; illa suis conditur inde locis.
o fortunatae sortis finisque uolucrem,
cui de se nasci praestitit ipse deus!
o felix, seu mas seu femina siue necutrum,
felix quae Veneris foedera nulla coit!
165 mors illi Venus est, sola est in morte uoluptas:
ut possit nasci, appetit ante mori.
ipsa sibi proles, suus est pater et suus heres,
nutrix ipsa sui, semper alumna sibi.
ipsa quidem, sed non eadem est; eademque nec ipsa est,
170 aeternam uitam mortis adepta bono.

appearance and the rich-hued bird from Phasis. Its size the winged thing that springs from the Arabs' land is scarce able to match, whether wild animal it be or bird. Yet it is not slow like large-sized birds which are of sluggish movement by reason of their heavy weight, but it is light and swift, filled with a royal grace: such is its bearing ever to the eyes of men. Egypt draws nigh to greet the marvel of so great a sight and the crowd joyfully hails the peerless bird. Straightway they grave its form on hallowed marble and with a fresh title mark both the event and the day. Every breed of fowl unites in the assemblage: no bird has thoughts of prey nor yet of fear. Attended by a chorus of winged creatures, she flits through the high air, and the band escorts her, gladdened by their pious task. But when the company has reached the breezes of ether unalloyed, it presently returns: she then ensconces herself in her true haunts. Ah, bird of happy lot and happy end to who God's own will has granted birth from herself! Female or male she is, which you will — whether neither or both, a happy bird, she regards not any unions of love; to her, death is love; and her sole pleasure lies in death: to win her birth, it is her appetite first to die. Herself she is her own offspring, her own sire and her own heir, herself her own nurse, her own nursling evermore — herself indeed, yet not the same; because she is both herself and not herself, gaining eternal life by the boon of death.

93

(ii) Ambrose's *Hexameron*, Bk. V, ch. 79-80

[from *Corpus Scriptorum Ecclesiasticorum Latinorum*, vol. xxxii, pars 1 (1896), pp. 197-8]

Phoenix quoque auis in locis Arabiae perhibetur degere atque eam usque ad annos quingentos longaeuam aetatem producere. quae cum sibi finem uitae adesse aduerterit, facit sibi thecam de ture et murra et ceteris odoribus, in quam impleto uitae suae tempore intrat et moritur. de cuius umore carnis uermis exsurgit paulatimque adolescit ac processu statuti temporis induit alarum remigia atque in superioris auis speciem formamque reparatur. doceat igitur haec auis uel exemplo sui resurrectionem credere, quae sine exemplo et sine rationis perceptione ipsa sibi insignia resurrectionis instaurat. et utique aues propter hominem sunt, non homo propter auem. sit igitur exemplo nobis quis auctor et creator auium sanctos suos in perpetuum perire non patitur, qui auem unicam perire non passus resurgentem eam sui semine uoluit porpagari. quis igitur huic adnuntiat diem mortis, ut faciat sibi thecam et inpleat eam bonis odoribus atque ingrediatur in eam et moriatur illic, ubi odoribus gratis faetor funeris possit aboleri?

Fac et tu, homo, tibi thecam: expolians te ueterem hominem cum actibus suis nouum indue. theca tua, uagina tua Christus est, qui te protegat et abscondat in die malo, uis scire quia theca protectionis est? pharetra inquit mea protexi eum, theca ergo tua fides; imple eam bonis uirtutum tuarum odoribus, hoc est castitatis, misericordiae atque iustitiae et in ipsa penetralia fidei suaui factorum praestantium odore redolentia totus ingredere. ea te amictum fide exitus uitae huius inueniat, ut possint ossa tua pinguescere et sint sicut hortus ebrius, cuius cito suscitantur uirentia. cognosce ergo diem mortis tuae, sicut cognouit et Paulus, qui ait: certamen bonum certaui, cursum consummaui fidem seruaui. reposita est mihi corona iustitiae. intrauit igitur thecam suam quasi bonus phoenix, quam bono repleuit odore martyrii.

In the regions of Arabia there is reported to be a bird called the phoenix. This bird is said to reach the ripe old age of 500 years. When the phoenix realizes that he is coming to the end of his life, he builds himself a casket of incense, myrrh, and other aromatic plants, into which he enters and dies when his time has come. From the moisture proceeding from his flesh he comes to life again. In the course of time this bird puts on 'the oarage of his wings' until he is restored to his primitive form and appearance. By the very act of his resurrection the phoenix furnishes us a lesson by setting before us the very emblems of our own resurrection without the aid of precedent or of reason. We accept the fact that birds exist for the sake of man. The contrary is not true: that man exists for the sake of birds. We have here an example of the loving care which the Author and Creator of the birds has for His own saints [cf.Ps.15.10; Acts 13.35]. These He does not allow to perish, just as He does not permit in the case of one sole bird when He willed that the phoenix should rise again, born of his own seed. Who, then, announces to him the day of his death, so that he makes for himself a casket, fills it with goodly aromas, and then enters it to die there where pleasant perfumes succeed in crowding out the foul odour of death?

You, too, man, should avail yourself of a casket: 'Strip off the old man with his deeds and put on the new.' [Col.3.9,10]. Your casket, your sheath, is Christ who protects and conceals you in the day of evil. Do you wish to be convinced that it is a casket of protection? 'In my quiver he hath hidden me,' [Isa.49.2] Scripture declares. The casket, then, is your faith. Fill it with the goodly aroma of your virtues, that is, of chastity, compassion, and justice, and immerse yourself wholly in the inmost mysteries of faith, which are fragrant with the sweet odours of your significant deeds. May your exit from this life find you clothed with that faith, so that 'your bones may be made fat' [Prov.15.30] and 'be like a watered garden,' [Isa.58.11] thus coming to life and flourishing. Be aware, therefore, of the day of your death, as the Apostle Paul realized when he said: 'I have fought the good fight, I have finished the course, I have kept the faith. There is laid up for me a crown of justice.' [II Tim.4.7,8] Like the good phoenix, he entered his casket, filling it with the sweet aroma of martyrdom.

95

(iii) The Vespasian Anglo-Saxon text of the *Phoenix*
[based on R Warner's *Early English Homilies*, EETS o.s. 152, (1917), pp.146-8]

Sanctus Johannes geseh ofer garseg swylc hit an land wære. Þa genam hine se ængel and gebrohte hine to neorxenewange. Neorxenewange nis naðer ne on heofene ne on eorðe. Seo boc sægð þæt Noes flod wæs feowrtig fedmen heh ofer þa hegesta dunen þe on middenearde synden, and neorxenewang is feowrtig fedme herre þone Noes flod wæs. And hit hangeð betwonen heofonen and eorðen wunderlice, swa hit se Eallwealdend gescop. And hit is eall [*fol*.166v] efenlang and efenbrad. Nis þære naðer ne dene ne dune. Ne þære ne byð ne forst, ne snaw, ne hagel, ne reign. Ac þær is *fons uite*, þæt is lifes welle. Þonne Kal*endas Januarii* inn gað þonne flowð seo welle swa fægere and swa smoltlice, and na deoppere þone mann mæig gewæten his finger on forewarde ofer eall þæt land. And swa gelice ælce monðe, ane siðe þonne se monð inn cumð, seo welle onginð flowen. And þær is se fægere wudeholt, þe is genemmed Radion *saltus*. Þær is ælc treow swa riht swa bolt and swa heh þæt nan eorðlic mann ne geseh swa heh, ne seggen ne cann hwilces cynnes heo synden. Ne fealleð þær næfre leaf of, ac heo byð singrene, wlitig and wynsum, welena unrim. Neorxenewange is upprihte on eastewearde þisse wurlde. Nis þær ne hete ne hunger, ne þær niht nefre ne byð, ac simble dæig. Sunne þær scineð seofen siðe brightlycor þone on þissen earde. Þær wuneð on Godes ængles unrim mid þan halgen sawlen oðð do[*fol*.167r]mes dæig.

Þær wuneð on an fugel fæger, Fenix gehaten: he is mycel and mære swa se Mihtige hine gescop. He is hlaford ofer eall fugelcynn. Ælcere wuca ane siðe se fægere fugel hine baðeð on þære lifes welle; and þonne flihð se fugel, and gesett uppe þæt hegeste trow ongean þære haten sunne. Þonne scinð he swa sunneleome, and he gliteneð swilc he gyldene seo. His feðeren synden ængles feðeren gelice. His breost and bile brihte scineð fægere and fage; feawe synden swylce. Hwat! his eagene twa æðele synden swa clæne swa cristal and swa scire swa suneleome. His fet synden blodreade begen and se bile hwit. Hwæt! se fægre

St John saw that it was like an island across the sea. Then the angel took him and brought him to Paradise. Paradise is neither in heaven nor on earth. Scripture says that Noah's flood was forty fathoms above the highest mountains on earth, and Paradise is forty fathoms higher than was Noah's flood. And it hangs wondrously between heaven and earth, just as the Almighty created it. And it is as broad as it is long throughout. There is there neither valley nor mountain. There is there neither frost, nor snow, nor hail, nor rain. But there is *fons uite*, which is the Well of Life. When the month of January comes in, then the well flows so pleasantly and so gently, and no deeper over all that land than a man may wet the tip of his finger. And similarly once every month, when the month comes in, the well begins to flow. And there is there the fairest grove which is called Radion *saltus*. Every tree there is so straight as a bolt and so high that no earthly man has seen a tree so high, nor can say to which species it belongs. Leaf never falls there, but it is evergreen, bright and winsome, of countless wealth. Paradise is directly overhead in the East of this world. There is there neither heat nor hunger; nor is it ever night there, but perpetual day. There the sun shines seven times more brightly than on this land. There a countless number of God's angels dwell with the holy souls until the Day of Judgment.

Therein dwells a beautiful bird called Phoenix: he is great and glorious as the Almighty created him. He is lord over all fowl-kind. Once a week the beautiful bird bathes himself in the Well of Life; and then he flies and occupies the highest tree facing the hot sun. Then he shines like a sunbeam and he glistens as if he were golden. His feathers are like angels' feathers. His breast and bright bill shine fair and multicoloured — there are few such. Lo! his two noble eyes are as clear as crystal and as bright as a sunbeam. His feet are both blood-red and the bill white. Lo! the beautiful bird flies from his land which is called fair Phoenix. Then he truly dwells in Egypt for

fugel fliðð of his earde, se þe is fægere Fenix gehaten. Þonne wuneð he witodlice on Egiptelande fiftene wucan feste togædere. Þonne cumeð him to, swaswa to heora kinge, fægeninde swyðe eall þæt fugelcinn; and fægere gegreteð ealle Fenix, writigeð and singeð ealle abuten him. Ælc [fol.167v] on his wisen, ealle hine herigeð. Þonne ferð þæt folc feorrene, swyðe wafigeð and wundrigeð, wylcumigeð fenix. 'Hal beo þu, Fenix, fugele fægerest! Feorren þu come. Þu glitenest swa read gold, ealra fugela king, Fenix gehaten.' Þonne wyreceð heo of wexe and writeð Fenix and meteð hine fægere þær se madme stant. Þonne fagenegeð þære fugeles ealle fægere and fage; feale togædere fealleð to foten. Fenix greteð. His stemne is swa briht swa beme, and his sweora swylce smete gold; and his forebreost fægere geheowed swylce marmelstan mæres cinnes. And him on read heow rudeð on þan hrynge. Goldfelle gelic gliteneð Fenix.

Þonne færð eft se fugel fægere to his earde emb fiftene wucan, and fugeles manige ealle him abuten efne ferden ufene and nyðene, and on ælce healfe oððet heo nehiget neorxenewange. Þær inn gefærð Fenix fugele fægerest, and eall oðer fugelcinn to heora earden gewændeð. Nu sæigð [fol.168r] her Sanctus Johannes soðcn worden, swa se wyrhte cann, þæt æfre binnen an þusend wintren þynceð Fenix þæt he forealdod seo, gegadered togædere ofer eall Paradis þa deorwurðe boges and heapeð tosamne. And þurh Godes mihte and þære sunneleome se heap byð onæled. And þonne fealleð Fenix on middan þæt micele fyr and wurð forbærned eall to duste. Þonne on þan þriddan dæge ariseð se fægere fugel Fenix of deaðe and byð eft edgung and færð to þære lifes welle and baðað hine þærinne. And him wexeð on feðeren swa fægere swa heo æfre fægerest wæren. Þuss he deð æfre binne þusend wintren: he hine forbærnð and eft edgung uppariseð. And næfð he nænne gemaca, and nan mann ne wat hweðer hit is þe karlfugel þe cwenefugel bute God ane. Þes halge fugel is Fenix gehaten, wlitig and wynsum, swa hine God gescop. And þuss he sceal drigen Drihtenes wille, se þe is on heofone heh and halig, ealra kinge King. Crist us generige þæt we on wynne wunigen mote mid þan þe leofeð and rixeð a bute ænde. Amen.

98

fifteen weeks together. Then, just as to their king, all that fowl-kind come to him, rejoicing very much; and all greet Phoenix pleasantly, chirping and singing around him. They all glorify him, each in his own way. Then folk from afar go to him; very much astonished and amazed, they greet Phoenix. 'Hail Phoenix, most beautiful of birds! Thou art come from afar. Thou shinest like pure gold, king of all birds, called Phoenix.' Then they make a monument from wax and write Phoenix and paint it beautifully where it stands. Then all the lovely, multicoloured birds there rejoice; many together falling at the feet of Phoenix, greeting him. His voice is as clear as a trumpet, and his neck like pure gold; and his breast beautifully formed like marble of an excellent kind. And his back is covered with a reddish hue. Phoenix glistens like gold foil.

Then the beautiful bird afterwards goes to his land about fifteen weeks and many birds, from above and below, and on either side, accompany him until they draw near to Paradise. There the fairest bird Phoenix enters and all the other fowl-kind return to their lands. Now here St John declares truly, as the Creator knows, that always within a thousand years it seems to Phoenix that he is grown old; he gathers all the precious boughs in Paradise and heaps them together. And through the power of God and of that sunbeam, the heap is kindled. And then Phoenix falls in the middle of that great fire and is completely consumed to dust. Then on the third day the beautiful bird Phoenix rises from death and is afterwards young again and goes to the Well of Life and bathes himself therein. And feathers grow on him as beautiful as if they had always been the loveliest. He does so always within a thousand years: he is himself consumed by burning and afterwards rises young again. And he does not have any mate and no man knows whether he is the male or the female bird except God alone. This holy bird is called Phoenix, lovely and pleasant as God created him. And thus he shall enjoy the desire of God who is high and holy in heaven, King of all kings. May Christ deliver us so that we may dwell in joy with Him who lives and reigns forever without end. Amen

Appendix 2
(i) F G Carmody's Y version of the Latin *Physiologus*

xxix De panthere

Propheta dicit: Factus sum *sicut leo domui* Juda, et *sicut panthera domui* Effraim [Os.5.14]. Panther hanc naturam habet: omnium animalium amicus est, inimicus autem draconi; omnimodo uarius est sicut tunica Ioseph [cf. Gen.37.3], et speciosus. Etenim dixit Dauid in XLIIII psalmo: Adstitit regina a dextris tuis in uestimento deaurato operta uarietate [Ps.44.10]. Panther quietum animal est, et mitissimum nimis. Si autem manducauerit, et satiatus fuerit, ilico dormit in fouea, et tertio die surgit a somno (sic et saluator noster). Panther autem, si surrexerit de somno tertio die, exclamat uoce magna, et de uoce eius omnis odor bonus aromatum; et qui longe sunt et qui prope, audientes eius uocem, assequuntur bonum odorem uocis eius.

Dominus noster et saluator surgens a mortuis omnibus bonus odor factus est nobis [cf. II Cor.2.15], his qui longe et qui prope, pax [cf. Eph.2.17]; sicut apostolus Paulus dixit. Multifarie sapientie dei [cf. Eph.3.10], hoc est uirginitas, abstinentia, misericordia, fides, caritas, unianimitas, pax, gaudium, longanimitas [cf. Gal.5.22]. Omni amore uaria est celestis sapientia dei Christi; bene de panthere dictum est, quoniam inimicus est draconi in acqua. Nihil ergo sine intentione intellectus de uolatilibus et animalibus diuine scripturae dixerunt; quoniam ait apostolus de satanan: Non enim eius *uersutias* ignoramus [II Cor.2.11], ambulat omni uia non bona [cf. Hier.2.23, 6.16].

Of the Panther

The prophet says: I have become like a lion towards the house of Judah and like a panther to the house of Ephraim [Hos.5.14]. The panther has this nature: it is a friend to all animals but an enemy to the dragon; it is multicoloured like Joseph's coat [cf. Gen. 37.3], and beautiful. For David said in Psalm 44: The queen covered in golden raiment of varied hues stood on your right hand [Ps. 44.10]. The panther is a peaceable animal and very gentle indeed. Now, once it has eaten and is sated, straightway it sleeps in a pit and on the third day it arises from sleep (just like our Saviour). The panther, then, once it has arisen from sleep on the third day, cries out in a loud voice and from its voice comes every good and fragrant smell, and those who are far and those near, hearing its voice, follow the good scent of its voice.

Our Lord and Saviour, rising from the dead, has become for us all a good smell [cf. II Cor.2.15], and peace for those far and those near [cf. Eph.2.17]; just as the Apostle Paul said: Various are the wisdoms of God [cf. Eph.3.10] namely virginity, abstinence, mercy, faith, charity, concord, peace, joy, longevity [cf.Gal.5.22]. The heavenly wisdom of the Lord Christ is varied with every kind of love; well is this said of the panther, since it is the enemy of the dragon in the waters. Indeed, the divine scriptures say nothing without point about flying creatures and animals; for the Apostle said concerning Satan: we are not ignorant of his tricks [II Cor. 2.11]; he walks in every way which is not good [cf. Jer.2.23,6.16].

xxx De ceto id est aspidoceleon

Phisiologus autem dixit de ceto quoddam, quod est in mari, nomine aspidoceleon uocatur, magnum nimis, simile insule, et plusquam harena grauis, figuram habens diabuli. Ignorantes autem naute, alligant ad eum naues sícut ad insulam, et anchoras et palos nauis configunt in eo; et accendunt super eum ignem ad coquendum sibi aliquid; si autem excaluerit cetus, urinat, descendens in profundum, et demergit omnes naues. — Sic et tu, o homo, si suspendas te et aligas teipsum in spe diabuli, demergit te secum simul in gehennam ignis.

Aliut naturale habet cetus: si autem esurierit, multum adaperit os suum, et omnis odor bonus per os eius procedit; odorantes autem pusilli pisciculi, secuntur eius odorem, et conponant se in ore magni ceti illius; cum autem impletum fuerit os eius, concludit os suum, et gluttit pusillos omnes illos pisciculos, hoc est modicos in fide. — Maiores autem et perfectos pisces non inuenimus adpropiare ad cetum: consummati enim sunt perfecti; etenim Paulus apostolus dixit: Non enim eius *uersutias* ignoramus [II Cor.2.11]. Iob perfectissimus piscis est, Moises et reliqui alii prophete; Ioseph effugiit cetum magnum, principis cocorum mulierem, sicut in Genesis scriptum est [cf. Gen.39]; sicut et Thecla Thamyridum, sicut Susanna duos senes Babylonicos iniquos; Hester et Iudit effugerunt Artaxersen et Olofernem; tres pueri Nabuchodonosor regem, magnum cetum; et Sarra filia Raguelis Nasmodeum (sicut in Tobia). Bene ergo Phisiologus dixit de aspidoceleon ceto magno.

Of the Whale that is the Asp-turtle

The Physiologus, then, has said something about the whale, named 'asp-turtle', which lives in the sea; it is very large like an island, and, heavier than sand, has the form of the devil. But ignorant sailors moor their ships to it as if to an island and fix in it the anchors and stakes of the ship; and they kindle fire on it to cook something for themselves; when, however, the whale has warmed up, it dives, descending into the depths, and submerges all the ships. Thou also, O man, if thou makest thyself dependent upon hope in the devil and bind thyself to him, he drowns thee with him at once in the fire of hell.

The whale has another nature; when it is hungry it opens wide its mouth and every good smell emanates therefrom. Then tiny little fish, smelling that, follow its scent and congregate together in the mouth of that huge whale; when its mouth is full, it shuts its mouth and swallows all those tiny fish — that is, those of little faith. We do not find the larger, mature fish hastening towards the whale: the mature are those endowed with perfection; for the Apostle Paul said: We are not ignorant of his tricks [II Cor.2.11]. Job is a most perfect fish and so is Moses and all the other prophets. Joseph escaped from the great whale — the wife of the chief cook — as it is written in Genesis [Gen.39], just as did Thecla from Thamyris and Susanna from the two wicked Babylonian elders; Esther and Judith escaped from Artaxerxes and Holofernes; the three boys from King Nebuchadnezzar, the great whale; and Sara, daughter of Raguel, from Nasmodeus (as in Tobit). Well, therefore, did the Physiologus speak of the great whale, 'the asp-turtle'.

xxxi De perdice

Hieremias dixit de perdice quoniam: Clamauit perdix, colligens que non peperit [Hier.17.11]. Perdix aliena oua calefacit laborans et nutriens; si autem creuerint pulli, et uolare coeperint, unumquemque genus euolans fugit ad parentes proprios, et solam eam dimittunt.

Sic et diabulus capit genus paruulorum; cum autem uenerint in mensuram aetatis, ueniunt ad Christum et ad ecclesiam, et fiet ille insipiens; hodie, si quis est in malis moribus, crastinum fiet ut sit sobrius; et fugisti diabulum, hoc est perdicem, et uenies ad parentes tuos iustos et prophetas et apostolos.

Of the Partridge

Jeremiah said this of the partridge: The partridge cried out, sitting on a clutch that it did not produce [Jer.17.11]. The partridge warms alien eggs, hatching and rearing them; when the chicks grow, and begin to fly, each and every kind flies for refuge to its own parents, and leaves the partridge alone.

Thus the devil captures the race of young creatures; but, when they come of age, they come to Christ and to the Church, and he will be foolish. If one follows evil habits today, he will be temperate tomorrow. Thou didst escape the devil, that is the partridge, and will come to thy true parents, the prophets and apostles.

xxiii Panthera

Est animal quod dicitur panthera, uarium quidem colore, sed speciosum ualde, nimis mansuetum. Physiologus dicit de eo, quoniam inimicum solum draconem habet. Cum ergo comederit et satiauerit se diuersis uenationibus, recondit se in speluncam suam, ponit se, et dormit; post tridum exsurgit a somno, et statim emittit rugitum magnum; simul autem cum rugitus exit de ore eius odor suauitatis, ita ut superet omnia aromata. Cum ergo audierint uocem eius omnes bestiae quae prope sunt et quae longe, congregant se omnes et sequuntur suauitatis odorem qui exit de ore eius; solus autem draco, cum audierit uocem eius, timore contrahitur, et fulcit se in terraneis cauernis terrae, ibique non ferens uim suauitatis odoris: in semetipsum contractus obtorpescit, et remanet ibi immobilis atque inanis tamquam mortuus; caetera uero animalia sequuntur pantheram quocumque uadit.

Sic et dominus noster Iesus Christus, uerus panther, omne humanum genus (quod diabolo captum fuerat et morti tenebatur obnoxium) per incarnationem ad se trahens: Captiuam duxit captiuitatem [Eph.4.8], sicut dicit Dauid propheta: Ascendeus in altum coepisti captiuitatem, accepisti dona in hominibus [Ps. 67.19]. Panthera enim omnia capiens interpretatur: sicut dominus deus noster (ut diximus), uidens humanum genus a daemonibus captum et idolis mancipatum atque omnes gentes et populos praedam diaboli effectos, descendens de caelis eripuit nos de potestate diaboli, et sociauit nos bonitati suae; et pietatis paternae filios apportauit, et impleuit illud quod propheta ante praedixerat: Ego (inquit) *sicut panthera factus sum* Effrem, et *sicut leo* domui Iudae idolis seruiebat [Os.5.14].Ergo tunc uocationem gentium et Iuadaeorum significabat.

Et animal uarium est panthera, sicut dictum est per Salomonem de domino Iesu Christo [Sap.7.22], qui est dei sapientia, spiritus intelligibilis, sanctus, unicus, multiplex, subtilis, mobilis, certus, *incontaminatus*, uerus, suauis, amans bonum, *aptus*, qui nihil boni

Panther

There is an animal that is called the panther, multicoloured indeed, but very beautiful and very gentle. The Physiologus says of it that it is the enemy of the dragon only. So when it has eaten and sated itself with various game, it hides itself in its cave, lies down, and sleeps. After three days it rises from sleep and emits straightway a great roar. At the same time as the roar, a sweet smell issues from its mouth, so that it overpowers all other scents. So, when they hear its voice, all the animals, those nearby and those far away, gather together and follow the sweet smell which issues from its mouth. Only the dragon, when it hears its voice, shrinks with fear, and fortifies itself in earthen caves in the ground and cannot endure the power of the sweet smell there. Shrunk within itself, it becomes paralysed and remains there immobile and useless as if dead; but the other animals follow the panther wherever it goes.

So also our Lord Jesus Christ, the true panther, drawing to Him by His incarnation the whole human race (which had been taken captive by the devil and held in subjection to death), led captivity captive [Eph.4.8]. Thus says the Prophet David: Ascending on high, Thou hast led captivity captive; Thou hast received gifts among men [Ps.67.19]. For 'panther' is to be interpreted as 'all-capturing': so our Lord God (as we have said), seeing the human race held captive by devils and enslaved by idols and all nations and peoples made the prey of the devil, descending from the heavens, snatched us from the power of the devil and made us partners in His excellence. He made us the sons of His father's goodness, and fulfilled that which the prophet had previously foretold: I (he said) have been made like a panther to Ephraim and like a lion to the house of Judah which served false gods [Hos.5.14]. Thus, then, he signified the calling of the Gentiles and the Jews.

And the multicoloured animal, the panther, is just as it is said by Solomon of the Lord Jesus Christ [Wis.7.22], who is the wisdom of God, the spirit of reason, holy, unique, diverse, fine, nimble, sure, uncorrupted, true, sweet, loving the good, apt, the

107

uetat fieri, clemens, firmus, stabilis, securus, *omnia potens*, omnia prospiciens, omnia faciens, mobilior sapientis, et reliqua.

Quod autem diuina sapientia Christus sit, testatur doctor ueritatis Paulus dicens: Nos autem praedicamus Christum crucifixum, Iudaeis quidem scandalum, *gentibus* uero stultitiam, ipsis autem uocatis Iudaeis atque gentibus Christum dei uirtutem et dei sapientia [cf. I Cor.1.23].

Et quia speciosum animal est panthera dicit Dauid de Christo: Speciosus forma prae filiis hominum [Ps.44.3]. - Et quia mansuetum animal est nimis Isaias dicit: *Gaude et laetare*, filia Sion, praedica filia Hierusalem, quoniam rex tuus uenit tibi mansuetus et saluans [Esai. 62.11]. — Et quia cum manducauerit et satiatus fuerit, statim quiescit et dormit, ita et dominus noster Iesus Christus, postquam satiatus fuit a Iudaeicis illusionibus. — id est a flagellis, alapis, iniuriis, contumeliis, spinis, sputis — manibus in cruce suspensus, clauis confixus, felle et aceto potatus, insuper et lancea perforatus: his igitur tot et tantis Iudaeicis muneribus satiatus, Christus obdormiuit et requieuit in sepulchro et descendit in infernum, et religauit illic draconem magnum et inimicum nostrum.

Quod autem die tertio exsurgit a somno illud animal et emittit rugitum magnum et flagrat odor suauitatis ex ore eius, sic et dominus noster Iesus Christus tertia die resurgens a mortuis, sicut dicit psalmista: Excitatus est tamquam dormiens dominus, tamquam potens crapulatus a uino [Ps.77.65]. Et statim exclamauit uoce magna ita ut audiretur in omni terra exiens sonus eius [Ps.19.5], in fines orbis terrae uerba illius, dicentis: *Gaudete* etiam et nolite timere, quoniam ego uici mundum [Ioh.16.33]; et iterum: Pater Sancte, quos dedisti mihi, custodiui; et nemo ex eis periit nisi filius perditionis [Ioh.17.12]; et iterum: *Vado* ad patrem meum et patrem uestrum, et ad deum meum et ad deum uestrum [Ioh.20.17]; et iterum: Veniam ad uos, et non *dimittam* uos orphanos [Ioh.14.18]. Et in fine euangelii ait: Ecce ego uobiscum sum omnibus diebus usque ad consummationem saeculi [Matt.28.20].

108

preventer of ill, merciful, firm, stable, free of anxiety, omnipotent, omniprescient, omnifacient, swifter in wisdom, etc.

Paul, the teacher of truth, testifies, however, what the wisdom of Christ is, saying: We, then, preach Christ crucified, a scandal indeed to the Jews, and an idiocy to the Gentiles. But, to those who have been called, both Jews and Gentiles, Christ is the power of God and the wisdom of God [cf. I Cor.1.23].

And since the panther is a beautiful animal David says of Christ: Beautiful in form beyond the children of men [Ps.44.3]. And since it is a most gentle animal Isaiah says: Rejoice and be glad, daughter of Zion, announce, daughter of Jerusalem that thy gentle king comes bringing salvation to thee [Is.62.11]. And since, when he has eaten and has been satisfied, he at once rests and sleeps, so also our Lord Jesus Christ, after He had been sated by Jewish ridicule, (that is by whips, blows, injuries, insults, thorns, spittle, hung by His hands on the cross, pierced with nails, having drunk gall and vinegar, and also been pierced by a lance), so, having been sated by such great and numerous Jewish gifts, Christ went to sleep and rested in the tomb and descended into hell, and there He bound the great dragon, our enemy.

But, as on the third day that same animal arises from sleep and emits a great roar and the smell of sweetness flames from his mouth, so also our Lord Jesus Christ, arises from the dead on the third day, as the Psalmist says: The Lord has awoken like one asleep, like a powerful man noisily drunk with wine [Ps.77.65]. And straightway He called out in a great voice so that His sound, issuing, might be heard in the whole land [Ps.19.5], His words to the limits of the circle of the earth saying: Rejoice also and fear not, for I have conquered the world [John 16.33]; and again: Holy Father, those thou hast given to me I have guarded and none of them has perished except the son of perdition [John 17.12]; and again: I go to My Father and your father and to My God and to your God [John 20.17]; and again: I shall come to you and I shall not leave you bereft [John 14.18]. And at the end of the Gospel He said: Behold I am with you every day until the end of the world [Matt.28.20].

Et sicut de ore pantherae odor suauitatis egreditur, et omnes qui prope sunt et qui longe (id est Iudaei, qui aliquando sensum bestiarum habebant, qui prope erant per legem; et gentes, qui longe erant sine lege), audientes uocem eius, repleti et recreati suauissimo odore mandatorum eius, sequuntur eum, clamantes cum propheta et dicentes: Quam dulcia faucibus meis eloquia tua, domine, super mel et fauum ori meo [Ps.118.103]. De his odoribus mandatorum eius dicit Dauid: Diffusa est gratia in labiis tuis, propterea benedixit te deus in aeternum [Ps.44.3]. Et Salomon in Canticis Canticorum dicit de eo: Odor unguentorum tuorum super omnia aromata [Cant. 4.10]. Unguenta enim Christi quae alia esse possunt, nisi mandata eius, quae sunt super omnia aromata. Sicut enim praesens aromatum species reddit odorem suauitatis, sic et uerba domini, quae de ore eius exeunt, laetificant corda hominum, qui eum audiunt et sequuntur. *Vnguentum exinanitum* nomen tuum, propterea adolescentulae dilexerunt te [Cant.1.3]; et: *Attraxerunt* te post se; et in odorem unguentorum tuorum *currimus* [Cant.1.4]; et paulo post: Introduxit me rex in *cubiculum* suum [Cant.1.4]. Oportet nos quam citius sicut adolescentulas, id est renouatas in baptismo animas, post unguenta mandatorum, Christi currere, de terrenis ad caelestia transmigrare, ut nos introducat rex in palatium suum, id est in Hierusalem ciuitatem dei et in montem omnium sanctorum; et cum meruerimus intrare illuc, dicamus: Gloriosa dicta sunt de te, ciuitas dei [Ps.86.3]; sicut audiuimus, ita et uidimus in ciuitate domini uirtutum [Ps.47.9]. Bene de panthera Physiologus dicit.

And just as a smell of sweetness issues from the panther's mouth and all who are near or far (that is, the Jews who once had the instinct of animals, who were near through the law; and the Gentiles who were far off, being without the law) hearing His voice, filled and restored by the most sweet smell of His commandments, follow Him crying with the prophet and saying: How sweet to my throat are Thy words, Lord, above honey and honeycomb to my mouth [Ps.118.103]. Concerning the smells of His commands David says: Grace is sprinkled on thy lips, therefore God has blessed thee for ever [Ps.44.3]. And Solomon in the Song of Songs says of it: The smell of thy unguents is above all spices [Cant.4.10]. As for the unguents of Christ, what else can they be but His commandments, which are above all spices? For just as the literal kind of spices give back the odour of sweetness, so the words of the Lord which issue from His mouth gladden the hearts of men who hear Him and follow Him. Thy name is an unguent poured forth; therefore young girls love Thee [Cant.1.3], and: They drew Thee after them and we run to the smell of Thy unguents [Cant.1.4], and a little after: The King has brought me into His chamber [Cant.1.4]. We ought to run as swiftly as young girls (that is, souls renewed in baptism), after the ungents of Christ's commandments, to pass from the earthly to the heavenly, so that the King may bring us into His palace (that is, into Jerusalem, the City of God, and to the mountain of all the saints). And when we have deserved to enter that, let us say: Glorious things are spoken of thee, City of God [Ps.86.3]; just as we have heard, so have we seen, in the city of the Lord of powers [Ps.47.9]. Well does the Physiologus speak of the panther.

111

Est belua in mare quae dicitur graece aspidochelone, latine autem aspido testudo; cetus ergo est magnus, habens super corium suum tamquam sabulones, sicut iuxta littora maris. Haec in medio pelago eleuat dorsum suum super undas maris sursum; ita ut nauigantibus nautis non aliud credatur esse quam insula, praecipue cum uiderint totum locum sicut in omnibus littoribus maris sabulonibus esse repletum. Putantes autem insulam esse, applicant nauem suam iuxta eam, et descendentes figunt palos et alligant naues; deinde ut coquant sibi cibos post laborem, faciunt ibi focos super arenam quasi super terram; illa uero belua, cum senserit ardorem ignis, subito mergit se in aquam, et nauem secum trahit in profundum maris.

Sic patiuntur omnes qui increduli sunt et quicumque ignorant diaboli astutias, spem suam ponentes in eum; et operibus eius se obligantes, simul merguntur cum illo in gehennam ignis ardentis: ita astutia eius.

Secunda eius beluae natura haec est: quando esurit, aperit os, suum, et quasi quemdam odorem bene olentem exhalat de ore suo; cuius odorem, mox ut senserint minores pisces, congregant se intra os ipsius; cum autem repletum fuerit os eius diuersis piscibus pusillis, subito claudit os suum et transglutit eos.

Sic patiuntur omnes qui sunt modicae fidei, uoluptatibus ac lenociniis quasi quibusdam odoribus diabolicis adescati subito absorbentur ab eo sicut pisciculi minuti; maiores enim se continent ab illo et neque appropiant ei. Sic ergo qui Christum semper in sua mente habent, magni sunt apud eum; et si sunt perfecti, agnoscunt multiformes astutias diaboli, et custodiunt se ab eo et magis resistunt: ille uero fugit ab eis [cf. Iac.4.7]. Dubii autem et modicae fidei homines, dum uadunt post uoluptates et luxurias diaboli, decipiuntur; dicente scriptura: Vnguentis et uariis odoribus delectantur, et sic confringitur a ruinis anima. [Prou.27.9].

Asp-turtle

There is a monster in the sea which is called *aspidochelone* in Greek but 'asp-turtle' in Latin. The whale is large indeed, having over its hide as much sand as there is by the sea-shore. This creature raises its back above the waves in the middle of the ocean so that it is believed by passing sailors to be none other than an island, particularly when they see all that place amply covered with sand as on all sea-shores. Then, thinking it to be an island, they lay their ship against it, and, disembarking, fix stakes and moor the ships. Then, in order to cook their food after their labours, they make hearths there on the sand as if on land. But when the monster feels the heat of the fire, it suddenly plunges into the water and drags the ship with it into the depths of the sea.

Thus suffer all who are incredulous and who, not recognizing the devil's stratagems, place their hope in him and tie themselves to his works. Straightway they are plunged with him into the burning fire of hell. Such is his cunning.

The second trait of that monster is this: when it is hungry it opens its mouth and from its mouth issues a certain sweet-smelling odour. As soon as the smaller fish are aware of that smell, they gather together inside its mouth. When its mouth is filled with the various little fish, it closes its jaws suddenly and swallows them.

Thus suffer all who are of little faith. Fed by pleasures and allurements represented by those diabolical smells, they are suddenly consumed by him like the tiny little fish; for the larger ones hold themselves back and do not approach him. Thus those who always have Christ in their minds are great in His sight; and, if they are perfect, recognize the manifold tricks of the devil, guard themselves from him, and strongly resist him. He, indeed, flees from them [cf. James 4.7]. But doubters and men of little faith, while they pursue the pleasures and lusts of the devil, are ensnared. As the Scriptures say: They are delighted by unguents and various odours and thus the soul is crushed in ruin [Prov.27.9].

113

xxv Perdix

Est uolatile quod dicitur perdix, fraudulentum nimis, sicut dicit sanctus Hieremias propheta de eo: Clamauit perdix et congregauit quae non peperit, faciens sibi diuitias non cum iudicio; in dimidio autem dierum eius relinquent ea, et in nouissimis suis erit stultus [Hier.17.11]. Physiologus dicit satis astutam esse perdicem, quae aliena oua diripiat, hoc est perdicis alterius, et corpore foueat; sed fraudis suae fructum habere non posse, quia cum duxerit pullos alienos, amittit eos; quoniam ubi uocem matris suae audierint, quae oua generauit, statim euolant et conferunt se ad suos parentes naturales; quodam munere adepto atque amore derelicto ille qui incassum in alienos suos fundit labores, et fraudis suae pretio multatur, remanet stultus et solus inanis.

Huius imitator est diabolus, qui generationes creatoris aeterni rapere contendit; et, si quos insipientes et sensus proprii uigore carentes aliquo modo potuerit congregare fouet eos illecebris corporalibus; at ubi uox Christi audita fuerit a paruulis, sumentes sibi alas spiritales per fidem, euolant et se Christo commendant, qui statim eos potissimo quodam paterno munere et amore sub umbra alarum suarum ipse suscipit, et matri ecclesiae dat nutriendos.

Partridge

There is a very deceitful bird called the partridge, as the holy prophet Jeremiah says about it: The partridge cried out and gathered together that which it had not produced, making for itself riches unrightfully; these will leave it in the middle of its days and at its end it will be a fool [Jer.17.11]. The Physiologus says that the partridge is very full of trickery. It snatches away alien eggs (that is, of another partridge) and warms them with its body; but it cannot possess the fruit of its deception, because when it has nurtured the alien chicks, it loses them. For when they hear the voice of their mother, who produced the eggs, straightway they fly away and gather to their natural parents. He who wastes his labours fruitlessly on those not his own and is penalized as the price of his fraud, remains foolish, alone and purposelerss, when he has lost a gift and abandoned love.

The devil is an imitator of him, striving to seize the offspring of the eternal Creator. If he can gather by any means any who are simple and lacking the vigour of their own sense, he cherishes them with fleshly allurements. But when Christ's voice is heard by the little ones, they take on spiritual wings through faith and fly off, entrusting themselves to Christ, who, straightway, with a mighty fatherly love and gift, takes them under the shadow of his wings and gives them to be nurtured by Mother Church.

To Miki

Best Wishes

for a

Happy Birthday

love.

Chris x